GOD'S INTRIGUING QUESTIONS

60 New Testament Devotions

Revealing Jesus's Nature

Book II

ENDORSEMENTS:
GOD'S INTRIGUING QUESTIONS

As those who minister to marriages, we know the value of asking questions. The Millers help us identify God's unique and powerful way of involving the hearts of others through questions. *God's Intriguing Questions* invites both individuals and couples to explore the Bible in a new, thought-provoking way.

—**Bill and Pam Farrel**, Co-directors of Love-Wise and authors of 50 plus books including bestselling *Men Are Like Waffles, Women Are Like Spaghetti*

The power of a question to transform our lives is undeniable. But its ability to open our eyes to matters of the heart isn't a result of reading the question, it's the result of responding. Larry and Kathy take us on a journey of discovery, question by question, beginning in the Garden of Eden and ending in Revelation. Honed in on matters of the heart, they highlight God's questions and invite us to reflect and respond. If you are seeking a devotional guide leading you to consider where you may have false thinking or hidden motives, while you get to know the God of the Bible, *God's Intriguing Questions* is a perfect choice.

—**Luann Budd**, Pastor's wife, Author of *Journal Keeping-Writing for Spiritual Growth* and President of the Network of Evangelical Women in Ministry (NEWIM.org)

This creative work by Kathy and Larry Miller allows God to gently invade our lives as we spend time with favorite Bible friends—Joshua, Elijah, David, Solomon, Job, Peter, Paul and many others. Through their experience and the questions God presents, we reflect on wise teaching and apply it to our personal circumstances and understanding of our Creator—his nature and his ways. A unique and powerful exploration of God's character and our response to his omnipotence.

—**Dianne Barker**, speaker, radio host and author *I Don't Chase the Garbage Truck down the Street in My Bathrobe Anymore!*

When things happen in this life we don't understand, we often ask God big questions. "Why did this happen? What does this mean?" Authors Kathy Collard Miller and Larry Miller take a bold new approach to questions in this devotional by looking not at our own questions for God, but the powerful questions God asks his people. Kathy and Larry offer a fresh look at Scripture to help readers discover the purpose of God's questions and what they mean for us today. I will enjoy reading this devotional again and again.

—**Kristine Brown**, Pastor's Wife, Speaker, and Author of *Over It. Conquering Comparison to Live Out God's Plan.*

When God asks a question, it isn't because he needs information. So why does he ask so many questions? The intriguing selections in this devotional are well-chosen. We found the insights regarding what God is revealing about our motives and his character very helpful. Moreover, the unique perspective of this devotional spurred us to go beyond the questions themselves into broader discussions of the Bible.

—**Bob and Roxann Andersen**, Authors, *The Marriage Dance*

This new type of devotional by Larry Miller and Kathy Collard Miller is intriguing. This husband and wife team examine the questions God asked throughout the Old and New Testaments and finds practical and current applications to our modern lives. They give biblical insights and personal examples that inspire and encourage readers to consider what questions the Lord may be asking them right now. This devotional could be read individually or by couples because Larry and Kathy's fifty-year marriage adds depth, insight, and evidence of the changes that can happen when we answer the questions the Lord is asking. This book can transform lives and inspire us to turn our hearts and homes toward Him.

—**Ron and Nancy C. Anderson**, certified marriage mentors and hosts of Growing Healthy Marriages at HSBN. TV. Nancy is the author of *Avoiding the Greener Grass Syndrome*

God's first question to Adam, "Where are you?" to among his last, "Do you love me more than these?" reminds us of the Lord's desire for us to meditate deeply about our life in him. Kathy Collard Miller and Larry Miller have gathered compelling questions to guide the reader on a 100-day journey through the Old and New Testaments requiring us to reach beyond our intellect to our spirit within. Each compelling quick-read chapter will strengthen your faith.

—**Deb DeArmond**, Christian author of books on marriage and family, including the humorous devotional, *Bumper Sticker Be-Attitudes*. http://debdearmond.com

If you are looking for a wake-up call to kick start your day, look no further. The Millers have nailed it when it comes to putting our lives in the hands of the one and only dependable God. The words of this book will enlighten, refresh, and bring you to a better understanding of why God tells us, "Seek me and you shall find me."

—**Tammy Whitehurst**, Motivational Speaker, Co-owner of the Christian Communicators Conference.

In this bold examination of a little explored aspect of God's character, Kathy Collard Miller and Larry Miller reveal the breadth and length, height and depth of the love of our Creator who longs to engage with us in conversation.

—**PeggySue Wells** is the bestselling author of twenty-nine books including *The Slave Across the Street*, *Chasing Sunrise*, and *Homeless for the Holidays*

Questions arrest our attention, probe our innermost thoughts and motives. Get ready for the great questions of life from the One who gives life. Insightful and practical, rooted in the Bible, and masterfully written, Larry and Kathy lead you on a 100-day journey (Books 1 and 2) from Genesis to Revelation. This book is a keeper.

—**Dave and Joanne Beckwith**, authors, *I Love the World, It's People I Can't Stand*, Authors and Regional Directors, StandingStone Ministry

I've been told I ask a lot of questions. I'm in good company. Throughout Scripture, God asks questions. In seeking our hearts and minds, we discover what lines up with God's heart and mind, and what needs to change to become more like him. Husband and wife duo, Larry and Kathy Collard Miller, explore this topic in *God's Intriguing Questions*. Fair warning, these questions get right down in your business. I highly recommend you take your time with this book. Don't simply read it, but let it be a mirror into your soul. You will come away from it transformed.

—**Kathy Carlton Willis**, God's Grin Gal, author and speaker

God's Intriguing Questions takes us through the Bible by showing us the questions God asked and how those questions relate to our own lives. A fascinating approach to learning more about the nature of God, this devotional book is well-organized and thought-provoking. It opens our minds to an often-overlooked feature in the Bible, God's questions, that too easily we dismiss as relating to the biblical character and not to ourselves. But why did he ask those questions, if he didn't want them to pertain to us all? I highly recommend this book as not only a devotional, but an in-depth personal Bible study.

—**Marilyn Turk**, multi-published author

GOD'S INTRIGUING QUESTIONS

60 New Testament Devotions

Revealing Jesus's Nature

Book II

KATHY COLLARD MILLER
LARRY MILLER

PUBLISHING THE POSITIVE

ELK LAKE PUBLISHING INC
Plymouth, Massachusetts

Cover and Interior Design: Derinda Babcock
Editor(s): Susan K. Stewart, Deb Haggerty

Author Represented by Suzy Q Media

PUBLISHED BY: Elk Lake Publishing, Inc., 35 Dogwood Dr., Plymouth, MA 02360, 2020

Library Cataloging Data

Names: Miller, Kathy Collard and Miller, Larry (Kathy Collard Miller and Larry Miller)

God's Intriguing Questions: 60 New Testament Devotions Revealing Jesus's Nature / Kathy Collard Miller and Larry Miller

272 p. 23cm × 15cm (9in × 6 in.)

Description: 60 Devotions from the New Testament revealing Jesus's nature and his love for us by the questions he asked in the Bible

Identifiers: ISBN-13: 978-1-951970-68-0 (paperback) | 978-1-951970-69-7 (trade paperback) | 978-1-951970-70-3 (e-book.)

Key Words: devotional, Christian living, God's nature, motives, God's qualities, God's questions, Bible study, devotions

LCCN: 2020938614 Nonfiction

DEDICATION

We dedicate our book to our pastor and his wife, David and Laura Palmer.

We appreciate your wise leadership, example of Christ, and supportive friendship.

TABLE OF CONTENTS

FOREWORD
By Erica Wiggenhorn

Being suddenly awakened in the middle of the night jolts your senses. Passive slumber to hyperacuity in seconds. A handful of times my children entered our room in the throes of the darkness with tear-stained faces and grabbed my hand.

"What are you doing here, honey?" I quickly ask, wanting to know what they need. Are they ill? Frightened? Worried and unable to sleep? My mother instinct kicks in, and I want them to identify the problem so I can help fix it.

One of my favorite questions God asks in the Bible is in I Kings 19:9 when he says, "What are you doing here, Elijah?" In fact, God repeats the question a second time. God's fatherly care kicks in, helping Elijah to identify the problem and proving to Elijah he has a plan to fix it.

Elijah obeyed God faithfully. He yearned for God's people to obey God wholeheartedly. He fervently prayed for revival, and God answered his bold prayers on Mount Carmel bringing down fire from heaven and the people to their knees in repentance. Then disaster struck. Elijah tumbled down that mountain into a valley of despair. After witnessing God do the miraculous, Elijah found himself in misery. Israel remained under the wicked pagan rule of Jezebel and Elijah fled.

Hence God's question. "What are you doing here, Elijah?"

I think this is a question we ask ourselves as equally often as God asks it of us. What am I doing here? Is there even a point to all of this? Will circumstances ever change?

Or we get distracted by the cares of this world. We begin to go through life on autopilot, and God jolts us to our senses saying, "Yes, child, but what are you doing here?"

The ability to confidently answer this question of God's could drastically change our lives. Maybe that's why God asks the question twice. It's doubly important to answer. I would dare say that nearly all God's questions circle back to this one, "What are you doing here?"

The beauty of *God's Intriguing Questions* is it helps us answer that question of God's and many others he asks. He addresses the stirring within our soul, reminding us our presence here on earth holds great significance and we matter—to God, to his plan, to the world and to those we love.

I also think God's action after a person responds to his question sheds great insight into our Father's love and care for us. He wants us to identify the problem and what we need from him, because he is more than willing and able to offer it to us.

This is what he does for Elijah. He refutes Elijah's disillusionment, which is based on Elijah thinking he is the only one who has a desire for God. He graciously unites him with a servant, Elisha. He also tells Elijah how the circumstances regarding the rule of Israel will soon change, reminding Elijah of his sovereignty and timing in all things. Elijah's senses are awakened to a plan beyond what he can currently see.

As we meditate on God's questions in the Bible, and also on the way he acts following a person's response, he invites us to see his work in our lives. God's responses help us identify the problems in our lives, broaden our vision, and shift our perspective to a plan we cannot initially see and a power at work in and through us. All of God's questions remind us God draws near and cares about our circumstances and our feelings. He asks in order to answer.

If you've come across this book, I would dare think you have some questions of your own.

- How did I get here?
- Why am I going through this?
- Where do I go from here?
- What is the meaning of all of this?
- What am I doing here?

God desires to answer those questions, and this book is the perfect tool to hear him speak to you. As the Millers explore God's questions and the responses of those he is addressing, the ultimate questions within your very soul will be answered. Your faith in God's power and your trust in his goodness will reach heights unimaginable.

Through each of these daily questions, ask God to help you answer his questions, giving your life purpose and meaning beyond your daily run of the mill activities. Ask him to reveal his plan and power even in deep sorrow or jubilant joy. As you make your way through this life-giving book, listen carefully to God's ultimate question for you: What are you doing here?

Run to God as Elijah did, to the only One who can truly identify whatever difficulty you are facing and provide the power to persevere through it. God is awake, even in the middle of the night, waiting for you to grab his hand.

—**Erica Wiggenhorn**, Speaker & Author of *Unexplainable Jesus: Rediscovering the God You Thought You Knew*

ACKNOWLEDGMENTS

We are very grateful for the leadership of our publisher, Deb Haggerty, at Elk Lake Publishing, Inc. Deb, we praise God for your determination to glorify God and support your authors. Thank you for including us in your publishing family.

Our editor, Susan K. Stewart, has diligently and patiently helped us make this book the best possible. Without your skills, Susan, our work would not be as clear and powerful.

We love working with graphic designer (and an author herself) Derinda Babcock with her creative ideas. Thank you, Derinda.

A supportive agent like Shawn Kuhn is invaluable. Thank you, Shawn, for being available.

Thank you to Meghan Enefiok Essien, whose suggested title described our theme so well we used it!

Our greatest acknowledgment is extended to our gracious Heavenly Father who has accomplished his continuing work over many years. Ultimately, because of him, we have the privilege of representing him in his assignments. Thank you, Lord God Almighty, for the joy of serving you. Our desire is to bring you glory. We praise, honor, and love you.

INTRODUCTION

Has God ever asked you a question? Have you learned something about who he is and your own motives? Or maybe you've wondered why God asks questions at all. Have you noticed the many times God and Jesus, who is God the Son, ask questions in the Bible? Doesn't it seem rather unusual? After all, God knows everything. To his glory, God Almighty doesn't lack information, discernment, or understanding.

Therefore, why does he ask questions? Does he *need* to ask questions? For whose benefit does he ask questions? Those are questions we will ponder in this book of one sixty short devotions. We think you'll unearth a fascinating spiritual exploration of two topics we don't dig into enough: God's qualities and our motives.

We are going to discover God's questions reveal himself in all the amazing aspects of his nature—his love, grace, faithfulness, mercy, kindness, wisdom, and so many other incredible pure qualities. He desires to draw us into a more intimate connection with him by learning the truth about him. Then we will seek him more, trust him more, and obey him more often.

How we long to respond to his love in those godly ways. Yet, we struggle even when we try to convince ourselves and others God loves us. As we'll find out, God's questions cause us to stop and think, asking ourselves, *If I love God and know God loves me, why am I so angry? Why do I shut down my heart?*

Why am I discontent? Maybe there's a reason which reveals I don't trust God as well as I thought.

God knows the answers. His questions help us unravel our complicated heart motives. This must be true because God isn't trying to figure us out. He not only designed us; he already knows about every detail of every day of our lives. Psalm 139:1-2 tells us, "O LORD, you have searched me and known me! You know when I sit down and when I rise up; you discern my thoughts from afar."

We will see his desire to lovingly care about every detail of each day of our lives as we study how God interacts in the lives of biblical characters. Knowing full well, of course, through the ages we all would read the very same questions and the Holy Spirit would prompt our own hearts to acknowledge the invitation as it pertains to us.

In the Bible, God starts the process very quickly. It only takes three chapters into Genesis before God asks his first question. His inquiries continue throughout the Old Testament and, in Book 2, into the New Testament with Jesus being the equally adept Question Asker. And the questions never end. God is a question-asking God.

That's the two-fold purpose of these devotional books. In these one hundred devotions (40 OT and 60 NT), you'll find out more about God's incomparable perfect nature. Each reading will emphasize at least one attribute of God. You will also read about the possible motives of the person or group of people God addresses.

Often the hearer totally resists and rejects God's inquiry into their heart and mind. Or the person has an "ah-ha moment." The question from an all-knowing God is intended to help each one correct or expand or transform a belief about God and know more clearly God's guidance. We pray you'll realize at times you might not fully believe the truth about God as much as you think. And why you don't always trust and thus obey him. The desires of your heart will be revealed as if a spotlight has been shown into the corners of your heart.

To assist your heart transformation, we've included two self-exploratory questions at the end of each reading. One addresses who God is, and the other helps you apply what you've studied. Then, we close with a simple prayer which focuses on praising and thanking God.

We have chosen to use the English Standard Version (ESV) for the quotes. We encourage you to understand the context of what is happening when God or Jesus asks a question by reading the full chapter or section it is in. Although we will try to give a sense of what is occurring, you will experience and understand the questions even more deeply and clearly knowing the background.

Because the Old Testament is primarily written in chronological order, we've listed the questions in that order. We will travel through the New Testament in the same way in Book 2. Thus, we will switch between the different gospel books and Acts to keep the story flowing more smoothly.

We have thoroughly enjoyed working on these books, and our own trust and knowledge of God's nature has grown tremendously. We pray a similar growth will be true for you as well.

—Kathy Collard Miller and Larry Miller

NEW TESTAMENT

In Book One, we looked at the questions God asked in the Old Testament. As we saw, some of those questions were technically from Jesus, who is God, appearing as the Angel of the Lord. But now we are looking at Jesus in the flesh while he walked the earth. His questions are recorded in the New Testament both in the Gospel accounts (Matthew, Mark, Luke, and John) and surprisingly in Acts.

Let's see how God Almighty wants to reveal himself through his Son Jesus who is God as a part of the Trinity along with the Holy Spirit. His questions will reveal his attributes and cause his listeners to evaluate their motives and their relationship with him. He longs for us to know him clearly, in truth, and intimately as we draw closer to him.

The questions we studied in the Book 1 were in the order as the Bible has them. In this section, we will take the questions from Matthew, Mark, Luke, John, and Acts in chronological order as they occurred in Jesus's life and ministry. The flow will assist our ability to understand the context of what is occurring throughout Jesus's life and after his resurrection. Remember, you will benefit the most if you have read the section surrounding the verse we are studying. We start when Jesus is twelve years old.

Why were you looking for me?

LUKE 2:49

Our three-year-old granddaughter loves to hide from me, Kathy, under the clothes racks as her mother shops. But one time, I couldn't find her. My heart raced as I envisioned someone taking her. *Oh, God, help me find her. Keep her safe.* In a few moments, she ran up to me giggling. I was both relieved and irritated.

Mary and Joseph must be experiencing the same panic when Jesus is missing. After the Passover festival, they travel toward home a full day before they realize Jesus isn't with anyone in their large caravan of relatives and friends. Turning back toward Jerusalem, they must be running at times, worried and scared.

Then Joseph and Mary find twelve-year-old Jesus in the temple—the last place they expect. He is sitting calmly, listening, and asking questions of the religious teachers. Mary's fear takes over and she chastises her son, in effect, blaming him for her worry. "Son, why have you treated us so? Behold, your father and I have been searching for you in great distress" (2:48).

We are like Mary. *God, you aren't showing up when I need you. I'm worried and it's your fault. Why do I have to hunt for you and wonder if I'll ever know your will?* Our fears swirl around in our minds. We forget God's work on our behalf in the past. Then when we come to our senses, we chastise ourselves for not trusting him.

The way to come to our senses and remember the truth is to think of the boy Jesus's response as he corrects his mother, "Did you not know I must be in my Father's house?" and as many versions word it, "at my Father's business?"

Mary says, "Your father and I have been searching for you." Mary downgrades her son's status as God who is also human to *only* human. In a sense, Jesus reminds her, "Yes, you are my human mother, but Joseph is not my father. He raised me in obedience to God, but God is my Father, and my identity will never change."

When we react in any way of fear, distrust, anger, lack of self-control—any time we are operating in the flesh and not being controlled by the Holy Spirit—we have downgraded God's qualities in our mind. He hasn't changed but our perception of him has in the moment.

Yet, God is forbearing and long-suffering. He has reasonable expectations of those in his human family. As we face problems challenging our trust in God's abilities to come through for us, God knows we will struggle. He is not deluded thinking we will someday "arrive" at perfection while on earth. He is with us for the long haul of a life-long process of sanctification.

We need not fear his impatience even though he corrects us and reminds us of his identity as everything perfect and everything we need.

- Do you ever believe the lie God shouldn't be forbearing with you? Why?
- What do you say about yourself when you fail? Can you find a verse speaking the truth about your God who won't give up on you?

Kathy Collard Miller and Larry Miller

My precious Lord, I praise you for your capability to be forbearing. Thank you for understanding my struggle and knowing how you will help me little by little.

What are you seeking?

John 1:38

Picture for a moment you are at a large conference. You are hungering to speak with the famous speaker who has already made a difference in your life through one presentation. During a break, you fearfully head to the front of the auditorium. *What do I say? Am I intruding?*

We can assume Andrew and John are feeling similarly. John, the writer of this gospel, leaves his name out. Both are disciples of John the Baptist when Jesus appears, therefore they must have seen when Jesus was baptized. Even their own teacher declares Jesus the sacrificial "Lamb of God" meaning Jesus is the Messiah who will be the sacrifice to take away sins.

Like approaching a famous speaker with trepidation, Andrew and John follow Jesus at a distance. And then the impossible occurs. Jesus turns around and "saw them following" (vs. 38). The answer to their longings.

John the Apostle uses the Greek word *θεασάμενος* *(theasamenos)* for "saw." This "saw" is not just a glance of disinterest. It means looking at closely and perceiving. Jesus's eyes bore into them. Each man must feel like his soul is revealed and known.

Then Jesus asks, "What are you seeking?" (vs. 38). Again, the wording is so powerful. In our world, this word "seeking" would be like "What are you searching for? What do you think will meet your needs? What are your expectations? What do you value?"

Such words point to heavy-duty heart examination of their motives. Jesus knows his Father has chosen them for the kingdom, so he goes for the jugular. They will not turn away from Jesus even though they will turn from John the Baptist.

They reply, "Where are you staying?" Again, we must look at the deeper meaning. "Stay" means remain or abide. They want to get to know him and spend time with him. Ironically, this points to a two-way street. Abiding with him now means him abiding forever in them through the Holy Spirit. But his indwelling will come later.

Jesus welcomes them warmly because their response indicates they are in touch with their deep needs. Unlike so many who have come to Jesus just wanting instant gratification through healing or solving their problem, these men want relationship. In an approachable manner, Jesus answers, "Come and you will see." The theme of "seeing" continues. They are seen and now they will see.

Jesus does the same for us. Jesus initiates an awareness of our need, our spiritual eyes are opened to our need, and then we "see" the need of continuing relationship. He welcomes us in order to reveal the longings of our hearts. He affirms our longings are valid because they are his method for creating our need for him.

Those longings to be loved, appreciated, approved, and respected must ultimately be met by God or through the people he chooses. He welcomes our need to "see" if we sincerely surrender to the ways he wants to meet them.

- How has God demonstrated to you his welcoming nature?

- In what way does he want you to welcome the needs of others, which will reflect God's nature?

Heavenly Father, I praise you for your welcoming nature, which responds to my needs. Thank you for meeting my needs in the best possible way for my good and your glory.

Because I said to you, "I saw you under the fig tree," do you believe?

John 1:50

Have you ever felt really known? Maybe someone who doesn't know you said something to you affirming your personality or calling. Every one of us longs to be fully known, loved, and appreciated.

Nathaniel experiences Jesus's affirmation. Jesus, a total stranger, identifies him as guileless, which means lacking deceit. Jesus tells him he saw him hidden under the fig tree. Jesus knows Nathaniel's nature, motives, and physical hidden location.

There are differing ideas of what Nathaniel is doing within the confines of the overhanging branches of the fig tree. Two in particular would seem to go along with Jesus's motive to convince Nathaniel the Messiah has arrived, and it is Jesus.

First, Nathaniel was meditating on or studying the story of Jacob's dream about angels going up and down the ladder in Genesis 28. Secondly, Nathaniel was seeking information from God about the coming Messiah.

Both go along with the Jacob story because Jesus is saying he, himself, is the predicted, symbolic ladder whereby people will have communication with heaven even though they are on earth. The gap between holy God and sinful man will be breached and the Messiah will destroy the power of sin separating man.

Nathaniel must think something like, *He is a stalker, saw me go under the tree, and I should reject what he says. Or, I must conclude he's the Messiah. I vote for Messiah. I'm in.* Nathaniel immediately calls Jesus the Son of God and King of Israel.

Jesus replies, in effect, "Then that's why you believe? Seeing and knowing you is nothing compared to what you are going to see and know, including the heavens opened and angels ascending and descending on the Son of Man."

Nathaniel's immediate response is thrilling to Jesus. Regardless of the various versions making Jesus's words a question or a statement, we must not "hear" it as Jesus expressing doubt, frustration, or rejection. He encourages Nathaniel in his new-born faith with a vision of the future.

Jesus also knows Nathaniel's response when Andrew told Nathaniel Jesus is from Nazareth (1:45). Nathaniel replied, "Can anything good come out of Nazareth?" (1:46). Why would Nathaniel be so prejudiced?

One conjecture is because the small town (maybe 2,000 people) of Nazareth has a Roman garrison, the Roman influence may have encouraged loose morals in the Jewish people. Regardless, many Jews have a critical opinion of Nazareth. Even though Nathaniel presumes Jesus can't possibly offer anything of value to him, Andrew's enthusiasm compels him to meet Jesus.

What a wonderful example for us as we respond to the new faith of new believers. They don't know a lot and we know how much more they should learn. Jesus encourages and affirms Nathaniel. He also doesn't try to immediately address Nathaniel's prejudice against Nazareth and himself. Jesus knows there is plenty of time for the Holy Spirit to change his heart and behavior. And for unbelievers, we can have patient grace in spite of their self-deception.

Jesus reveals his joyful nature in his response to Nathaniel's newborn faith. He doesn't overwhelm him with high expectations. We should do the same for others regardless of their knowledge. Jesus rejoiced over what Nathaniel did know, not what he didn't yet know.

- How does Jesus's joy over a new believer speak to you?
- How does Jesus's joy affect your response to a Christian who is weak in their faith?

Amazing God, I praise you for your joy over me regardless of my lack of knowledge. Thank you for encouraging me even though my faith seems small at times.

Woman, what does this have to do with me?

JOHN 2:4

In the English world, if we overhear a man call his mother "woman," we would be incensed. It seems disrespectful and even mean-spirited.

We can be assured Jesus uses the word as an endearment motivated by love and understanding. Why? Because as he later hangs on the cross carrying the weight of sin, he acknowledges his loving care for her using the same word. "Woman, behold, your son!" (John 19:26). He tells her his apostle John will provide for her. In both instances, "woman" is the same Greek word.

In John 2, the setting is the famous wedding at Cana. Mary cares about the horrible problem the groom and bride encounter. In Jewish weddings, which last seven days, running out of food or wine is a shameful mark against the family. Mary tells Jesus, "They have no wine." Whether she believes her son will provide miraculously or just be smart enough to find some more wine, we don't know, but she trusts Jesus can help. Good for her.

Yet Jesus says, "Woman, what does this have to do with me?" The meaning of this phrase as used in other places in the Bible is, "We aren't on common ground." Or "Your perspective is entirely different than mine." We can identify five ways they differ.

Motive. Mary desires to spare the couple embarrassment. Jesus desires his Father to be glorified.

Timing. Mary wants the wine problem to be solved immediately. Jesus knows the right timing includes providing anonymously.

Quality. Mary assumes he will merely replace the same kind of wine. Jesus provides something so superior the wedding coordinator is amazed.

Method. Mary tells the servants to do what he says. Even though she exhibits a measure of faith, she might also want to be involved. After all, Jesus can assure them himself; he doesn't need her. We don't know, but maybe she thinks she knows better. Jesus knows he can do anything and doesn't need anyone's help.

Feelings. Based on Jesus's comment, we must conclude she feels anxious. She may have taken on a responsibility not hers. One way to translate the Greek is, "What is that to me and to thee?", another way of saying, "It's not your responsibility, and it's not mine." Jesus is perfectly calm. He doesn't feel pressured by anyone, even his beloved mother. He will only do what his Father wants him to do which gives him peace, confidence, and guidance.

- Like Mary, we can bring our concerns and cares before God. Unlike Mary, we can trust God will do the perfect thing.
- Like Mary, we can have faith Jesus can do anything. Unlike Mary, we don't need to help him but only follow his directions.
- Like Mary, we can direct our tense feelings to God. Unlike Mary, we can feel peaceful and confident.

We can't criticize Mary because we are like her. Jesus understands she is an imperfect human, even if she is his mother. Jesus responds to us with equal understanding even as he calls us to deeper trust and godly living.

- What principles or other stories from the Bible support your assurance God is understanding?
- Who has represented God's kind of understanding to you? Who has been less than understanding?

Eternal God, I praise you for your understanding, which never expects me to be sinless. Thank you for providing my redemption and my empowering for growth in godliness.

Yet you do not understand these things?

JOHN 3:10

Nicodemus, the "teacher of Israel," comes to Jesus in the night whether because of fear of being seen with the rebel Jesus, or he wants an extended time with him without the crowds interrupting them. Or he doesn't want anyone to think he needs to be taught. After all, as a Pharisee in the Sanhedrin, everyone believes he knows everything.

He comes to Jesus with flattery. "Rabbi, we know that you are a teacher come from God, for no one can do these signs that you do unless God is with him" (3:2). He might be thinking, "I hope this covers up my feelings of inadequacy and neediness."

Notice Nicodemus doesn't ask a question but John 3:3 says, "Jesus answered him, 'Truly, truly, I say to you, unless one is born again he cannot see the kingdom of God.'" *Answered* him?

Jesus delves right into the question in Nicodemus's heart which the Pharisee most likely can't even formulate. He just knows his knowledge of the Law doesn't quench his spiritual hunger. Other Pharisees aren't willing to admit their striving for perfection isn't working. Or they believe it is.

The Greek word for "again" is a vague adverb with three possible meanings: born from the beginning, born a second time, or born from above. *Which door do you choose Nicodemus?*

And Nicodemus goes for the "earthly" door. *I must reenter my mom's womb,* which although is impossible, is a way of solving a riddle with human ingenuity. The door meaning "be born from above" will open revealing the fulfillment of the Law in a perfect heaven where there is no need to strive. But Nicodemus is depending upon the door of knowledge, not an eternal perspective.

Jesus replies, "If I have told you earthly things and you do not believe, how can you believe if I tell you heavenly things?" (v. 12). Jesus is saying, "You are wanting to solve your spiritual hunger with man-centered solutions. I am offering you a completely God-centered way because the Holy Spirit must make the new birth possible—'from above.' All your knowledge won't open the door for you into heaven, nor will your striving for perfection.

"You are at the first step, admitting your need. Now believe I am descended from heaven in a miraculous birth as foretold. Recognize my powerful Spirit must do the work just like the wind makes a difference. You can't control it. You only see the results. Your new life will result from my powerful work of a heart change, not more human effort."

Nicodemus must have made a heart commitment to Jesus because he later defends him before the Sanhedrin (John 7:50-51) and helps Joseph of Arimathea bury Jesus (John 19:39-40).

If you've ever shared with someone about the freedom of depending upon Jesus for salvation, yet were met with resistance, be comforted realizing only God is powerful enough to create a spiritual hunger. It's not up to you. It must be the Spirit moving in a heart.

- What situations of life most seem like God is not powerful enough to make a difference in your loved one's life?
- How could trusting God's power make a difference in the way you respond to someone?

My great God, I praise you for your power, which sees no obstacle, even the resistance of a human heart. Thank you I can trust your will is never thwarted or changed.

Give me a drink.

JOHN 4:7

Although the ESV does not denote this as a question, many commentators believe it is. Let's include it because we see another aspect of God's attributes.

As we study the Bible, we must remember Scripture was written without any delineation of chapters or verses. John writes on a continuous scroll so there is a sense of every word is a part of a greater whole. We come to the famous story of Jesus's encounter with the Samaritan woman remembering the context. Previously, John writes, "and [Jesus] needed no one to bear witness about man, for he himself knew what was in man" (2:25).

Then John, led by the Holy Spirit, thinks something like, "I'm going to write down the encounters Jesus had with different kinds of people. And each story will show how he knew the heart of every person. He valued every person, and he went to great lengths to reach each one as the Father directed." Jesus encounters many more people than the Gospel stories indicate but God leads John to include a few.

One example is the knowledgeable, law-keeping, and respected Nicodemus who recognizes his need. Then John includes the opposite, the Samaritan woman, an immoral woman who lives a life of shame and resists feeling needy. Nicodemus comes voluntarily to Jesus and in contrast Jesus seeks out the immoral woman. Jews hate Samaritans for forsaking true worship of Jehovah and for marrying non-Jews. They hate them so much they never step foot in Samaria.

Yet Jesus "had to pass through Samaria" (4:4). Though weary from his journey he goes out of his way to create this pre-ordained appointment with a needy woman. Jesus asks for water not out of need. He can instantly fill the well so high it overflows. But he knows the best way to approach this woman. Jesus shows his value of her by asking for help. She could help or say no. He is empowering her, a person who has had zero power in her life.

The ensuing conversation is a fascinating study of Jesus's ability to help her see the condition of her heart. What an encouraging Son of God.

From then on, the woman asks most of the questions and Jesus wisely responds in ways that continue the conversation until Jesus offers the golden opportunity. "The woman said to him, 'I know that Messiah is coming (he who is called Christ). When he comes, he will tell us all things.' Jesus said to her, 'I who speak to you am he'" (4:25-26).

She leaves her water pot, runs to tell the villagers who hate her saying, "He told me all that I ever did" (4:29). What freedom from shame. She is rehearsing her sin because she knows she is set free and is valuable to the Messiah. As a result, a whole town believes in Jesus, the "Savior of the world" (4:42).

What a contrast of characters, a learned ruler/Pharisee and an uninformed woman. Jesus knows "what was in the heart of men" and their great need. And with love and joy, he responds to their known and unknown hearts' cries.

- Who do you know who you think is the least likely to be wooed to salvation in Jesus?

- Is there someone who you never thought would become a Christian, but Jesus's invitation created their changed heart?

Loving God, I praise you for your encouragement to know you. Thank you for knowing the desires and need of every heart and responding in the right way.

Why do you question these things in your hearts?

MARK 2:8

Over the years there have been movies about one person able to read the thoughts of another. The plot develops as the person selfishly uses the ability for his own good, not others. Thankfully, God always uses his questions for the good of another.

The story behind Jesus's question this time is the heart-touching one of the paralytic's friends breaking through the roof to get him within healing distance of Jesus. They must think their friend needs to be close in order for Jesus to heal him, otherwise they could have called out from the blocked door or pounded on the roof. Instead, they take off the layers of wood, mud, and straw, whether with their bare hands or some implements. The roof is strong enough to walk on but not strong enough to resist the passionate, motivated love these men have for their disabled friend.

The bedridden man is finally before Jesus, and to everyone the need is obvious. A healing of his body. But Jesus says, "Son, your sins are forgiven." The friends intend only their friend's physical healing, but Jesus wants the healing of his soul. Jesus always sees beyond what we think is important. We can be healed physically in some way but if we are still being distressed by sin, we really aren't healthy.

The scribes question Jesus's action "in their hearts" (v. 6) because Jesus is blaspheming by claiming to be God who is the only one who can forgive sins. Blaspheming is a crime punishable by death. Jesus reveals their thoughts, and they must be totally shocked—just like the characters in a movie when another person refers to their thoughts. The scribes must also feel threatened because their evidence gathering mission is no longer secret. Jesus knows their intentions for his harm.

Then curiously Jesus asks, "Which is easier, to say to the paralytic, 'Your sins are forgiven,' or to say, 'Rise, take up your bed and walk'?" (2:9). He is revealing his authority on earth. No one can see whether the paralytic's sins have been healed, but when he stands up, everyone can see the physical healing. Jesus reveals three truths about himself: he heals the soul from sin, he heals the body from disease, and he points out lies corrupting the mind.

This story emphasizes Jesus's omniscience. Jesus is not surprised. He never has a "deer looking in headlights" stare. He never wonders what someone is thinking or guesses at their motives.

What wonderful assurance for our lives. Jesus the Son of God knows everything—including our deepest needs. He knows which need requires addressing first, second, and last. When we are receptive to his better plan, we can reduce the "questioning in our hearts." We aren't forced to hide our confusion. God knows every motive, thought, and hope of our hearts. He wants to work with us to bring understanding. He asks us to evaluate, "Why do I question God's ways in my heart?"

- Has anything happened to you seeming to indicate God is not omniscient?
- What seems scary or risky about honestly revealing the motives of your heart?

Healer Jesus, I praise you for your omniscient quality, which assures me nothing is hidden from you. Thank you for your authority to overcome every obstacle and to reveal your plan for my good.

Can the wedding guests mourn as long as the bridegroom is with them?

Matthew 9:15

You are at a wedding, and after the bride and bridegroom are pronounced husband and wife, the groom turns and with a solemn face announces, "Now we all will mourn. Don't expect any food at the reception, because we will be fasting."

You look around to see confused and sad looks on the guests' faces. A dirge fills the church as the bride and groom drag themselves down the aisle. After the dreary reception where there's no food, dancing, or singing, everyone is given a little baggie of dirt. As the newly married couple leave the reception, everyone throws dirt on them.

No way. And yet the metaphor is a modern explanation for the dialogue in Matthew's house. Although the setting is not a wedding feast, the gathering is definitely a party. Jesus, his disciples, and Matthew's party guests are feasting and having a great time. Even those terrible "tax collectors and sinners" (verse 11) are joining in—at Jesus's invitation. Can't you just envision Jesus having the biggest smile of all of them?

If anyone has trouble thinking of Jesus as being joyful, the proof is Galatians 5:22 where joy is included in the fruit of the Holy Spirit. Since the Holy Spirit is equally God in the Trinity, like Jesus, they all have the same nature, including joy.

But the disciples of John the Baptist aren't rejoicing. They look over the crowd with a judgmental scowl and demand, "Why do we and the Pharisees fast, but your disciples do not fast?" (9:14). Wow, they are on the prowl to let others know everyone should follow the rules like they do.

We can give John's disciples understanding grace because their teacher is in prison, and they are mourning. They think everyone should be mourning along with them because such a valuable vessel of God might be facing death. Jesus should especially be concerned and grieving, because John is his cousin. Plus, John launched Jesus's ministry as the Messiah back when John baptized him. Jesus should be more grateful for John's valuable support. Might they even be thinking Jesus wouldn't have been successful without John? We don't know.

Jesus interjects, "Can the wedding guests mourn as long as the bridegroom is with them?" (Matthew 9:15). Jesus reminds John's disciples of who he is, and at this period of time everyone should rejoice. He completely trusts his Father's plan for his cousin. Another reason is Jesus wants to enjoy the party because he is truly joyful in nature.

Jesus assures John's disciples they shouldn't worry because the day will come when he will be gone, and his own disciples will miss him and mourn (Matthew 9:15). Jesus's statement might be a gentle rebuke they shouldn't be jealous. Others are allowed to rejoice even when some are mourning.

Many theologians refer to John's disciples' emphasis upon fasting as the old covenant of keeping the Law to earn God's favor. Jesus represents a new covenant of grace free from performance. Of course, God will at times prompt Christians to fast, but there's a distinct difference in motive. The motive for fasting is one of joyful gratitude knowing they have a joyful Savior.

- What other words would you describe for God's joyful nature?
- If you find difficulty in thinking of Jesus as joyful, why do you think so?

Beautiful God, I praise you for your perfections, which include joy. Thank you for including joy as a fruit of the Spirit because it represents your Holy Spirit's nature in me.

Do you want to be healed?

JOHN 5:6

What an intriguing question to a man waiting to be healed. Our initial reaction is, "Of course he does. What are you thinking? Who wouldn't?" But the man responds, "Sir, I have no one to put me into the pool when the water is stirred up, and while I am going another steps down before me" (John 5:7).

The crippled man doesn't say, "Of course. Can you help?" He gives an explanation. Or is it an excuse?

After thirty-eight years of a debilitating disease, is he comfortable in his situation? What would it mean to be healthy again? Maybe he fears handling the responsibilities of normal life.

I wonder how often Jesus asks us a similar kind of question. By allowing frustrating circumstances, he might be asking: "Do you want to give up your disability of discontent?"

When someone hurts us, is he asking, "Do you want to be emotionally healed by relinquishing your bitterness?"

If someone takes advantage of us, is he asking, "Will you give up your victim mentality?"

Do we have standard reasons—or are they excuses—for our discontent, anger, and powerlessness? The waters of healing are right before us. Why don't we jump in?

Jesus is a wise counselor. He knows how to prod the handicapped man's heart and our own. Our hearts are an open book to him and a mystery novel to us. But he desires to reveal the pages which are stuck together with the glue of sin or fear.

Jesus is prying two pages apart as he gives the man an assignment *he can refuse*. "Jesus said to him, 'Get up, take up your bed, and walk.' And at once the man is healed, and he takes up his bed and walked" (5:8-9).

We are cheering as he is healed and obeys with no explanations or excuses.

Interestingly, Jesus tells him to "take up your bed." The man couldn't leave it there as his safety blanket in case he felt bad again.

Many years ago, I, Kathy, didn't know releasing my unrealistic expectations of Larry would be Jesus's way of asking me to burn my mat of bitterness. In our early marriage, Larry worked two jobs and had a flying hobby. He was rarely home and gave little help with our two children, one a newborn and a toddler. I wrapped myself in my mat of resentment as a way to protect myself from the pain of his rejection.

I, Larry, wrapped myself in my mat of controlling pride thinking Kathy had the problem, not me. In my view Kathy never appreciated my efforts so I gave up even trying.

We both at different times and in different ways heard Jesus ask, "Do you want to be healed?" The process of restoration began when we each stopped giving explanations and instead acknowledged our own self-centered spiritual sickness. We will celebrate our 50th anniversary in 2020 and are more in love with each other and Jesus than ever before.

Although we each sometimes try to pick up another mat, God persists saying, "Do you want to stay well?"

- God knows the intentions of your heart. Is that good news or bad news for you?

- Can you identify a time you were clueless to your motives and God prodded your heart to show you?

Wise Counselor, I praise you for your wise interest in my heart motives. Thank you for your gentle questions which help me examine my heart.

How can you believe, when you receive glory from one another?

JOHN 5:44

Jesus is addressing the Jews who are obsessed with the opinions of others who must think well of them, speak highly of them, and recognize their Law-abiding behavior. Because Jesus is exposing their sinful pride, they plan to kill him. They reject the fact only God is glorious. They think they should qualify. God's glory can be defined as the ultimate perfections of every one of his attributes. The religious leaders don't meet such a high standard. We've been seeing the contrast. Unlike everyone, including the religious leaders, every attribute of God is always perfect and exhibited in the best possible way.

Somehow in childhood we each begin to seek glory from other people to feel safe and considered good. We don't know how to believe God loves us even though we struggle and fail. Then we react to people who don't acknowledge our goodness in four primary sinful ways: anger, sadness/hurt, shame, and anxiety.

- I'm angry because you don't see me the way you should.
- I'm sad or hurt because you make me feel bad about myself.
- I feel ashamed because my imperfections are revealed for everyone to see.

- I'm anxious or fearful because I feel powerless to protect my reputation.

The degree to which we are angry, sad, ashamed, or anxious indicates the level of our dependence upon people's opinions. They must define us rightly becoming our god. We have forsaken our loving God's opinion of us who knows the truth about our imperfections and loves us regardless.

In contrast, Jesus says to the Jews—and to us— "I do not receive glory from people" (John 5:41). Therefore, Jesus can say to the Jews, "Look at me for your example to stop receiving glory from one another." His motive is to free them from their people pleasing and give them the joyful assurance of Jehovah's unconditional love for them. God's love is something they can't earn.

How does God want to set us free? John 5:30-38 gives us Jesus's insights as he uses himself as an example of truth:

v. 30: I can do nothing on my own

v. 30: I seek only God's will

v. 32: God will justify me and determine my value

v. 33: John has testified of me, not for my benefit but for yours. I don't need John's confirmation

v. 36: The glorious things I do are determined and empowered by my Father, not by my own power

v. 37: God's affirmation of me is enough for me

v. 41: I don't lay hold of the praise given me. I hear it but I don't accept it as defining me.

We can't comprehend fully a man who had absolutely no need for any human to think well of him. Jesus says, "I seek not my own will but the will of him who sent me" (John 5:30).

Jesus's motivating attitude is the key for diminishing people pleasing. We can more and more recognize we each have absolutely nothing to offer God or others. His power is the only source of any good work we do. Then our motive will be to reflect God's glorious perfections and not our own.

- How does meditating on God's glory motivate you to desire to diminish your people pleasing?
- How do you feel knowing God patiently works to diminish your people pleasing and doesn't expect you to be perfect until you reach heaven? Why do you think that's so?

Perfect God, I praise you for your glorious being, in which there is absolutely nothing imperfect in you. Thank you for being willing to use me even though I'm a weak and inadequate vessel.

Have you not read what David did when he was hungry?

I, Kathy, once traveled with a Christian speaker to an event and her philosophy of travel was completely different than mine. I carefully weighed my luggage to make sure I didn't exceed the limit to avoid extra charges.

My friend packed more luggage than mine and when I expressed concern she might be charged, she flippantly waved her hand, saying, "It'll work out." I was shocked she thought she didn't need to follow the rules. As she checked in, I stood too far away to hear the conversation, but she wasn't charged. I was angry. She didn't follow the rules and got away with it. No fair. Why can't I?

I would have made a very good Pharisee. I don't like people who don't follow the rules and then receive mercy or blessings.

If I had heard the Pharisees accuse Jesus's disciples of breaking the law for eating grain in the field on the Sabbath, I would have agreed and said, "Naughty, naughty. Play by the rules." Like Jesus's response to the Pharisees, Jesus would need to say to me twice, "Have you not read …" (Matthew 12:3, 5). I wouldn't receive the message the first time.

Jesus's questions urge them to see the Old Testament law as pointing to a coming Savior who would mercifully save those who can't keep the law perfectly. They think they keep the religious rules perfectly and gleefully point to others who don't. And besides, Jesus is greater than the laws designated in the Old Testament because he created them. He reminds them temple priests break the fourth commandment by "working" on the Sabbath. Jesus and his disciples are serving in the "temple" because the whole earth is the Savior's temple. Therefore, whatever he does is keeping the heart of the law—in order to bring blessings.

Jesus mercifully wants the Pharisees to recognize their added rules put an undue burden on the people God never intends. God's simple rules are supposed to help people live an abundant life, not make them believe God demands perfection.

My own motive for keeping the rules is similar. I want to know and keep the rules in order to avoid getting in trouble, not because I'm grateful for God's mercy. As a child, I even believed God symbolically stood over me with an axe waiting for me to do the wrong thing because he wanted to punish me.

I wrongly saw God demanding my perfection before I qualified for his unconditional, complete love. I couldn't see the good heart of the heavenly Father saying the rules point me to my need for a Savior. Jesus died on the cross because God could mercifully forgive and cleanse me. When I finally "heard" the wonderful news—the Gospel—I was set free from the bondage of the wrong interpretation of God's law. And I could extend grace to others more freely.

I'd like to think if I again travel with my "freeloading" speaker friend, I will be thrilled if she isn't charged. Just don't ask me to go so far as to not weigh my luggage.

• Why do you think God is eager to reveal his mercy?

- Are you more a law breaker or a law keeper? How do you think God wants to show you his mercy in your breaking or your keeping?

Merciful God, I praise you for your mercy, which you don't have to force yourself to exhibit. Thank you for extending to me a forgiveness I can never earn.

Is it lawful on the Sabbath to do good or to do harm, to save life or to kill?

MARK 3:4

The topic of anger can be confusing. How can God be angry and yet be good? We equate anger with harm and evil intent. This story of Jesus healing the man with the withered hand is the only time in the New Testament Jesus is described as angry. Of course, we think of the time when he cleansed the Temple of money changers, but the account does not use the word angry. We interpret his actions as angry, but his actions could also be done under complete control. His motive is always for good, to set his beloved people free from the injustice of the wicked religious system.

Anger in itself is not necessarily wrong. The key is the motivation energizing our reactions. Is the action done in patience or with evil intent? With a calm voice or with fury? Is the purpose for another person's good or their harm? To teach or to punish?

Jesus asks the Pharisees and scribes to think of the purpose of the Sabbath, which is to worship God and do good. Jesus asks a question to reveal truth, but they refuse to admit he is right. Their silence is rebellion. They know they are caught. The risk is too great. Jesus is stealing the hearts of the people away from them, and they are losing their status and power.

Over centuries the spiritual ruling position of the religious leaders grew because they convinced the Israelites only they knew God's will. The Law started with the Ten Commandments and then God detailed in Deuteronomy more specific directives. Over time when the Israelites would come to the priests and ask how to apply a particular command, the priests set up more detailed regulations, which grew into over six hundred nit-picky rules.

Teaching the rules took priority over encouraging the people to seek God and learn his grace and love, even if someone didn't perform perfectly. The priests took full advantage of the people's dependence upon them to explain things, lifting themselves up not only as experts but as perfect examples.

Jesus is threatening their status. He wants the people to seek God and grow spiritually dependent upon trusting God and following his will—even if they are imperfect. Jesus offers freedom and abundant living.

Sometimes we want to be told what to do rather than taking the time and effort to seek God's leading by studying the Bible for ourselves. But then we can be in bondage to the opinions of others. Jesus is sorrowful knowing his Father gives life, not the fear of what others think.

Ironically the Pharisees say Jesus shouldn't heal and do something good on the Sabbath. After Jesus heals the man, they are angry and plan along with their enemies, the Herodians, to kill Jesus. They are deceived by believing a lie about Jesus and self-focused wanting to protect their status.

We don't have to be like those officials. We can be empowered by the Holy Spirit to have righteous anger, motivated by wanting someone's good. And we can have godly sorrow, grieving for the hurt others are experiencing, like Jesus does.

- What has been your understanding of God's anger in the past? How do you imagine Jesus looked physically in this story?
- What have you learned about having sorrowful anger? What motive helps you have a godly anger?

Almighty God, I praise you for your wisely controlled nature, which is never out of control. Thank you for your calm response to me even when you discipline me and point out my disobedience.

If salt has lost its taste, how shall its saltiness be restored?

MATTHEW 5:13

Put yourself in the scene for a moment. You are sitting in a crowd staring longingly at Jesus, who in the manner of a rabbi is seated, most likely on a large rock. He's not standing. He has just said in the previous verses, 11 and 12, his followers should be glad when they are persecuted because they will receive a reward in heaven.

Keep in mind many small rebellious groups have already been crushed by the Romans. Being identified as leading or being involved in a rebellion against Roman rule is no small thing. It might mean persecution or death. As we listen to Jesus we may be thinking, "This is another small rebellion, but after all, change has to start somewhere. We must be delivered from the cruel dominion of the Romans. Maybe this Jesus will be the answer. I'm willing to do whatever it takes."

In those moments, could we possibly have a sense of the magnitude of what Jesus knows will happen? No. We can't see through the ages to understand Jesus's teaching of the Gospel, the "good news," is his sacrificial death for the forgiveness of sins and the restoration of the relationship between God and man. This wonderful message will spread throughout the whole world. The saltiness Jesus is referring to will reach every nation and develop a thirst for knowing God through the Messiah.

Jesus tells his listeners they are the salt of the earth, which means they have an incredible purpose as God's representatives. He is urging them to not lose their saltiness even if persecuted because his plans are greater than they can imagine.

Jesus always purposefully crafts his words. His reference to salt is clear to his listeners. There are three basic purposes of salt at that time: thirst, preservation, and seasoning. Jesus teaches his followers to first, create spiritual thirst in others. Secondly, preserve godliness in culture. And thirdly, season their actions with godliness so their fruitful lives seem attractive—"tasty"—to others.

If we stop or diminish those influences by not representing Jesus rightly, Jesus says in verse 13, our spiritual saltiness "is no longer good for anything except to be thrown out and trampled under people's feet."

Commentators believe Jesus might be referring to how salt, which was stored for holy purposes in the temple, could become unfit. As a result, the salt was sprinkled upon the roadways and possibly the steps of the temple to prevent the priests from slipping. Salt, which could have had a superior impact, basically became a kind of gravel. Jesus wants his followers to know he has much higher purposes for them than being used for gravel.

Knowing God is in charge of the result of our representation will comfort and strengthen us. Even when we represent him well, we can't force anyone to become spiritually thirsty, or culture be preserved, or our godly actions be attractive to others. God must work, even using us when we are persecuted. Thankfully, he graciously and generously wants to use us to be a part of his plan.

- What does it mean to you Jesus is generous to use you to make a difference in another's spiritual thirst?
- Can you think of a time you obeyed God's direction and he turned your obedience into something bigger than you expected?

Heavenly Father, I praise you for your generous nature in including me in your plans for the Gospel. Thank you for empowering me to reach out to others even if I'm persecuted.

For if you love those who love you, what reward do you have?

MATTHEW 5:46

Jesus is talking about a totally different kind of love contrary to what his listeners have been taught. It would be like someone telling you, "Do you want to go to Mars? I have one ticket left." *What? Are you kidding? That's dangerous. How do I know it's safe?*

The audience must be thinking the same thing. *Are you kidding? To love those who don't love me is dangerous. They will think they can take advantage of me. After all, then I should also love the Romans and those who help them like the tax gatherers. Jesus can't mean them or those who assist them. No way.*

Jesus digs into the motives of his listeners by asking, *What reward is there for loving those who love you? You know the tax gatherers fake liking you to get on your good side and then take your money. When you love others who love you, you are just like the tax gatherers. You love for selfish reasons. I'm asking you to love everyone, even to your possible detriment.*

Jesus's question is in opposition to the teaching of the Israeli rabbis and other religious leaders. The Pharisees use Leviticus 19:18 (at least part of it) to prove they don't need to love their enemies: "You shall not take vengeance or bear a grudge against the sons of your own people, but you shall love your neighbor as yourself: I am the Lord." And who do they teach are their "neighbors"? Other Israelis—except for their own people who are tax gatherers. Love everyone but *those* people—and the wicked Romans, of course.

Jesus challenges his listeners' unloving motives. They must be questioning; *I should love the guy who robs me when he overcharges my taxes? But then I won't be able to complain about him. I won't be able to feel superior to such a worm. Then I won't feel justified to hate.*

In the verse before Matthew 5:46, Jesus gives a crucial insight as we think of loving in scary ways. He says, "For he [God] makes his sun rise on the evil and on the good, and sends rain on the just and on the unjust" (vs. 45).

Jesus is saying, *I'm God and like my heavenly Father who is such a good God, we give common grace and blessings even to those who are unjust. Why can't you trust me to provide whatever you, my chosen ones, need as you face a scary, sacrificial opportunity? If I provide for those who don't honor me, won't I provide for you who is my favored one? You'll have enough love to share with others.*

At this point, those listening don't know anything about the great sacrifice their teacher will be making within a short time. But we do. We can tell ourselves, *If God loves me so sacrificially to provide salvation at such a high cost, then I can love others no matter the cost.*

Does it feel like you need to protect your heart by loving only those who can offer you something good in return? Trust God's unconditional love modeled for you through Jesus suffering the ultimate humiliation and sacrifice.

- In what way has God shown you his unconditional love?
- In what way is he asking you to love someone even though it seems risky in some way?

Generous God, I praise you for guaranteeing your loving nature will always take good care of me. Thank you for empowering me to love others as you love me.

Is not life more than food, and the body more than clothing?

MATTHEW 6:25

When we first met Herman, a big gray cat who was much beloved by his masters, John and Dixie, we knew he had a problem. Worry. If a little space in his bowl showed the bottom, even though his food was piled high around it, he paced back and forth mewing. A huge bag of cat food was only a foot away in the pantry, but he didn't believe John and Dixie would be generous enough to put more in his bowl.

Jesus knows we are all like Herman. Jesus admonishes his listeners in Matthew 6 to stop worrying by believing God is stingy when he is actually generous. He is *wisely* generous because he knows what's best for us and provides accordingly. He is *graciously* generous because he provides even though we don't deserve his gifts. And he is *powerfully* generous because there is nothing good he can't provide.

Think of it this way. You meet a billionaire who hands you a check for a million dollars. You are stunned. It'll take care of the current expenses of the mission hospital you support. Because of his generosity, you ask with no hesitation, "Could you also pay for the taxi to take me to the airport in an hour? It'll cost about twenty-five dollars."

The billionaire looks at you, starts wringing his hands, and says, "No, that's beyond my means."

If we worry, we are expecting God to reply the same thing. But Jesus says, "If I'm generous, capable, powerful, and loving enough to give you the spark of life, why would you doubt I can provide food to sustain your life? If I can wonderfully create your body by designing intricately every cell to work in sync, how could you not believe I'll protect your body with clothing? Trust me."

Right before Jesus asks his question, he says, "Therefore I tell you, do not be anxious about your life, what you will eat or what you will drink, nor about your body, what you will put on" (vs. 25).

The Greek word "anxious" is μεριμνα and translated "care, anxiety, and worry." The root is μεριζω meaning "to divide, to separate." When we worry, we have divided beliefs. We describe this fact as "railroad tracks." One of the tracks thinks, "God is generous. He'll provide." But the other track thinks, "But I should take care of it in case he doesn't." Or "But he didn't before—at least the way I thought he should."

The English spelling for μεριμνα is *merimna*. When I, Kathy, first saw the word, I wrongly read it as "meditate." But the two words can be related in our understanding. Someone has said if you know how to worry, you know how to meditate. The difference is what you are dwelling on. Worry is the result of meditating on the lies about God's holy character and specifically believing he is stingy. Faith meditates on God's faithful provision for our good even if he doesn't act the way we think he should.

Let's not be like Herman, the cat. Let's trust in the generous heart of our master.

- Is there an area of life where God doesn't seem generous? What does his seemingly lack of generosity look like?

- Can you recount a time when God unexpectedly revealed his generosity?

Loving God Almighty, I praise you for revealing your generosity through giving me life and a body, which no man can provide. Thank you for always knowing the best way to express your generosity.

Or which one of you, if his son asks him for bread, will give him a stone?

Matthew 7:9

I, Kathy, will never forget staying all by myself at my aunt and uncle's home for a few days. I was twelve. At my house I had a lot of responsibilities. Not at my aunt and uncle's. They had a pool, fed me, and I could do anything I wanted. Heaven.

On the day I left, my aunt handed me a box of See's candy. "This is for you." Wow. She definitely spoke my love language. Then I noticed an attached note, "For the Collards." I was shocked. I thought the gift was only for me. When I shared my confusion, she said, "Well, you'll know the candy is for you."

Disconnect. I didn't know how to process her words or if I should state my case, but I went home and shared the precious candy with my family. I confess I was bitter and didn't enjoy what I ate.

When I think of Jesus's question, I think of my disappointment about the candy. I thought I was receiving a delicious loaf of freshly baked bread but actually a hard stone lay in my hand. After also giving the analogy of a good father not giving a serpent when a child asks for fish, Jesus says, "If you then, who are evil, know how to give good gifts to your children, how much more will your Father who is in heaven give good things to those who ask him!" (7:11).

This is a "if that good thing is true, just think of this better thing" reasoning. If you aren't perfect as a parent yet give good gifts, just think what a perfect parent like your Father God will give you.

Jesus addresses the crowd close by the Sea of Galilee, who are primarily peasants who eat bread and fish. Jesus shows how responsive he is by referring to items and concepts these people experience every day. He doesn't talk physics or chemistry or how far it is to the moon. His responsiveness deals with their daily needs. He knows they, at times, feel like God doesn't answer their prayers. They conclude he isn't a good God. He must not want the best for them. Jesus counteracts the lie with this appeal to their normal parenting feelings. They deeply care for their children, and they would never consider mocking and deceiving their child by giving them something bad for them.

Don't you appreciate the way Jesus relates to them at their emotional and mental levels? My aunt knew what I cared about. Unfortunately, something within her wanted to cover all the bases and look good to everyone. My aunt was quite wealthy and could have afforded a box of candy for each of us in our family of five—easily.

I'm so grateful God is so far different than my aunt. Like nowhere in the same universe. Although the world defines good from a skewed perspective, Jesus always gives the best because he is responsive to our real needs, not what the world has convinced us is best for us.

- What synonyms would you substitute for responsiveness, especially as you think of God?
- Have you experienced something convincing you God isn't responsive to your cries for help or your needs? What is your belief now?

Compassionate God, I praise you for your sensitive responsiveness to my needs. Thank you for always knowing what's really best for me, even when I'm convinced something else is better.

Why do you call me "Lord, Lord," and not do what I tell you?

LUKE 6:46

I, Larry, can see how I falsely believed I could call Jesus my "Lord" because I received Christ as my Savior in middle school, but there was no deep spiritual foundation for the "house" of my life. Building a spiritual foundation would indicate I needed God. As a teenager, I'd experienced painful results when put in a weak position. I vowed I would never feel or be seen as weak. When Kathy and I married, I thought, *Ok, now I have a wife in the house, and it includes great benefits. She can build the foundation. I will secure a job to provide for the house. I think I will make a good police officer with my instinctive decisiveness. I'll apply.*

But in time, God tore down my self-confidence and rebuilt my spiritual house with a strong foundation of dependence upon him as my true Lord. Jesus continues the rebuilding, affecting for good my marriage, family, and ministry.

The Greek word for "LORD" is κύριε (*kyrie*) meaning master, supreme in authority, controller. The crowd hearing Jesus knows clearly the significance of a master who has supreme control over his servants and family. His word is law.

The religious leaders and even common Jews call Jehovah Lord but are unaware of the motives of their hearts. Jesus shares how his listeners can evaluate their motives and commitment. "Are you obeying my commands? Either your spiritual house has a deep foundation on a rock and stays firm in a flood, or it has no or a weak foundation and can be swept away in a flood" (our words of Luke 6:47-49).

His listeners know well the dangers of floods. In the winter, frequent violent storms create flooding. Buildings with no foundation can easily be washed away especially on the hills of Judea.

Likewise, the true test for our heart's commitment—a firm foundation—is when we're under stress. When life is calm and no "floods," we can easily depend upon ourselves even when we say Jesus is Lord. When the flood overwhelms us, our actions—any reaction opposite to the fruit of the Spirit (Galatians 5:22-23)—reveals the truth. Jesus isn't Lord.

Jesus isn't intending to bludgeon his listeners into an intolerable guilt but to help them face the fact their hearts and their motives may not be as pure as they think. He uses the example of a shaky foundation to express his love, not wanting them to be washed away by life's floods. If they recognize their need of a good Lord, he calls them to follow him. Then he will build a firm foundation on himself, the Rock.

Whether or not anyone in the history of the world acknowledges Jesus as Lord doesn't determine whether he is Lord over all the earth. God, Jesus, and the Holy Spirit are Lord of everything. Lordship is the nature of the Trinity's very being, which never diminishes, even when his created beings reject his Lordship.

- When you think of a lord, what is your immediate reaction? If it is negative, are you transposing those feelings onto God, the true, good Lord?

- How can submitting to Jesus's Lordship change one of your ungodly reactions to a godly one?

Master Jesus, I praise you for your Lordship, which is an intricate, permanent part of your being. Thank you for helping me understand how growing in trust in you as my Lord is actually the best thing I could ever be doing.

What did you go out into the wilderness to see?

LUKE 7:24

If you've ever experienced doubts about your salvation, then you will love the story of John the Baptist sending messengers to Jesus expressing his doubts. His two disciples ask Jesus, "Are you the one who is to come, or shall we look for another?" (Luke 7:19).

We can understand how John might be wondering. He is in prison and possibly depressed from bad treatment and fear for his life. He wonders if he made a mistake identifying Jesus as the Messiah because Jesus hasn't established the earthly kingdom overthrowing the Romans. Even John the Baptist is not expecting a spiritual kingdom. Of course, he wants Jesus to take over the government because as king he can then give a reprieve to John.

Although not all commentators agree, most say John's disciples have a private audience with Jesus. Jesus compassionately responds to the messengers without criticism of their teacher John. Instead he helpfully points out his miracles are fulfillment of Old Testament prophecies verifying he is the Messiah. But he explains he is not creating an earthly kingdom. John's messengers then leave to return to John.

As Jesus turns to the crowd, he could have used John's doubts as an object lesson, but he doesn't. Even though the crowd doesn't hear Jesus's words to the messengers, they must be curious about what was said.

Out of compassion for John's reputation, he uses the situation for an object lesson, which is far more important. He asks, "What did you go out into the wilderness to see? A reed shaken by the wind? … A man dressed in soft clothing? Behold, those who are dressed in splendid clothing and live in luxury are in kings' courts. … A prophet? Yes, I tell you, and more than a prophet" (Luke 7:24-26).

He reminds them John called them to repentance and transformation. He bucked against the system and made lots of enemies. Yet he stayed true to his calling.

The reference to reeds is a word picture of the reeds surrounding the Jordan River where John baptized them. Reeds sway but John didn't. What a wonderful example for them, even though Jesus knows John's faith is weak at this time.

Then Jesus makes the more important point. "Yet the one who is least in the kingdom of God is greater than he" (Luke 7:28).

John represented the Old Testament requiring sacrifices and keeping the law. But Jesus will establish a superior covenant with his death, resurrection, and the formation of his church. Aren't we who are on the other side of the cross the more blessed? We have the full assurance Jesus's death and declaration of "It is finished!" is enough. And the resurrection verifies the validity of the sacrifice.

Jesus assures the audience John fulfilled God's plan for him, but in effect, says, "You who believe will have more blessings in my new kingdom." Our God's assuring nature doesn't want us to doubt. But if we do, his compassion will steady us as Jesus did with John.

- In what different ways can you think God reveals his assuring nature or compassion, both Scripturally and in people's lives?
- How has God assured you recently even though you experience doubts about God and the Christian life?

Perfect Lord, I praise you for your gentle assuring nature which draws me to you. Thank you for having compassion on me who sometimes feels like a swaying reed.

How can you speak good, when you are evil?

MATTHEW 12:34

We knew we had to include a question like this one from Jesus. We've studied so many questions from Jesus sounding positive and revealing his gentle and compassionate nature. We must also study how he speaks forcefully and strongly and is still able to speak the truth in love. His nature is revealed as balanced.

In this passage Jesus calls the Pharisees a "brood of vipers." They have just accused him of blaspheming against God by using Satan/Beelzebul's power to cast out a demon. If Jesus indeed did that, he would be rebelling at the highest level.

In contrast, none of us with our impure motives should call anyone a "viper." Even if we convince ourselves we intend it for their good, words like those don't align with Scripture's commands (Ephesians 4:29). Only Jesus has pure motives. He knows the heart of the person and which words are right for their good.

Jesus uses the phrase "brood of vipers" to emphasize the motives of the Pharisees. Nothing but venom can be expected from a snake, and nothing but lies can be expected from selfish Pharisees who are committed to a religious philosophy, which gains them worldly position, power, and status.

Jesus uses strong words to get their attention and call them to repentance. He knows they won't (because he knows everything), but he is also aware of the listening crowd who is still trying to decide their allegiance. He must correct the lies the religious leaders are teaching.

The words Jesus uses lend themselves to the idea he is a hothead who is mean-spirited. Nothing could be farther from the truth. We can't hear his tone, but his desire is always to bring his listeners to repentance and belief in himself.

Jesus is also instructing those in the crowd to examine themselves by paying attention to the words they speak. He says, "For out of the abundance of the heart the mouth speaks. The good person out of his good treasure brings forth good, and the evil person out of his evil treasure brings forth evil" (Matthew 12:34-35). The Greek word for abundance means "what is left." Our words are an overflow of what our hearts trust in and what our minds believe.

God continues to sanctify Kathy and I, Larry, in this area. As someone who easily believes I know best, combined with my training as a police officer, I can make fast judgments of others. I am challenged to allow God's Spirit to empower me with compassion and understanding in the "overflow" of my words out of my motives. God is working. My uncaring reactions are diminishing. But my inconsiderate words still reveal a part of my heart distrustful of God's balanced nature.

If you are a Christian, even your improper words can't cause you to lose your relationship with God because your sins—past, present, and future—have been nailed to the cross. But God does want you to grow in your ability to speak balanced words being guided by the enlightenment of the Holy Spirit for the good of another.

- What does it mean to you to think of Jesus as "balanced?" What can block you at times believing in his balanced nature?

- In your current challenge, what might balance empowered by the Holy Spirit's power look like?

Incredible God, I praise you for your balanced wisdom to know everything and then act correctly every single time. Thank you for your desire to empower me to continue learning spiritual balance.

Who is my mother, and who are my brothers?

Matthew 12:48

This passage can be perplexing. A messenger comes into the packed house and interrupts Jesus. "Your mom and brothers want to talk to you." Jesus sweeps his hand across the crowd and asks his question, "Who is my mother, and who are my brothers?" Why would he not be responsive to his family? Family is important. In the cultures of the middle east like Israel, the family especially takes precedence over everything.

Exactly. Jesus is zealous for the family of God, his spiritual brothers and sisters. They take precedence over every other person or group and will last into eternity. God intends the earthly family to be a representation of the forever family in heaven, even if humans on earth can never be a perfect model. Jesus's response points to his zealous nature. He is fervent, ardent, devoted, and diligent.

On the golf course, we saw a mother quail grow twice as large in defense of her babies hiding in the bushes. A road runner came by and she strutted out with a fierce determination to protect her children. The road runner knew this was a mean mama and quickly scurried away. We knew we were watching zealousness in action.

As we think again of Jesus's reaction to his family, we must look at the evidence of their attitudes about Jesus and his ministry. Over time, they become true followers, but they didn't understand in the beginning.

The first mention besides Jesus's childhood is when Jesus, his disciples, and his family spend a few days together in Capernaum (John 2:12). The brothers try to tell him what to do (John 7:3-4). The brothers don't believe in him (John 7:5). The family wants to take custody of him thinking he is out of his mind (Mark 3:21). His mother is at the cross, and Jesus arranges his apostle John to care for her (John 19:26-27). The family is in the upper room after Jesus ascends into heaven (Acts 1:14). James, his half-brother, is a prominent leader in the early church (Galatians 2:9).

When his family sends a messenger into the room, commentators wonder if his family wants special favors. We can also easily imagine they feel ignored, replaced, and unimportant. Over time, how often did Mary reflect on the angel's words and the wonder of Jesus's birth to help her in all the uncertainty and especially at the cross? But obviously, at certain times, she is a typical mother desiring her son make the right choices.

Jesus uses this situation to teach a new idea. His human family represents his "old" family, Israel. But the disciples and followers are his "new" family, who will become a part of the church starting on the Day of Pentecost.

Just as a zealous God is passionate about all goodness and righteousness, Jesus is zealous to develop, protect, and control his spiritual family which will bring himself glory. If you know Jesus as your Savior, then you are a part of the Body of Christ, and God is zealous about you.

- When you think of God's zealousness, what example in nature comes to your mind and explain why.
- What aspect of being cared for by a zealous God is most meaningful to you?

Great God Almighty, I praise you for your zealousness about me and all your children. Thank you for your zealous passion in including me in your forever family.

Ought not this woman ... be loosed from this bond?

LUKE 13:16

This may sound ridiculous to point out, but Jesus is intelligent. His intelligence is obvious, yet do we give him credit for his intelligence or praise him for how smart he is? And do we recognize how he uses his intelligence?

Without realizing it, we may discard his intelligence by believing we know how he should work in the lives of everyone. The story in Luke 13:10-17 helps us to identify his creative intelligence. Jesus addresses two different kinds of bondage in two people who are entirely different. He works individually to offer each one life. One receives the gift; the other doesn't.

The first is a suffering woman who has been bent over for eighteen years. Jesus sets her free from her bondage, and she praises God. The second is a synagogue ruler who is in bondage to a wrong perspective about the Law. The ruler rejects freedom. Jesus responds to each one in exactly the right way, but the result is different.

The woman stands up straight. The ruler wants to remain bent over with the load of the Law.

The woman can't see the sky. She might as well be blind, but she has spiritual insights. The ruler is blinded by the good of the Law insisting Jesus be ruled by rules, which aren't the best for people.

The woman is filled with joy, able to walk without bumping into people. The ruler is disgruntled and unhappy. He fears losing the prestige, power, and authority to tell everyone how to keep the law. As a result, he pressures—bumps against—those he is supposed to assist.

The woman feels loved by Jesus through his identity of her as a "daughter of Abraham." The ruler pretends to be superior to those in his charge and feels terrible about himself.

Jesus wants to set them both free. He intelligently ministers to each one in an individual way, because he knows their authentic need. He works perfectly yet the response is the opposite.

We must remember Jesus's example when we minister to someone. Let us not be in bondage to assumptions and our own understanding how God should work. Just because God worked a certain way in our lives doesn't mean every other person will be impacted in the same way. Just because we follow God's leading as we minister, doesn't mean the outcome will be what we want and need. God is intelligent and can work through the power of his Holy Spirit individually, uniquely, and with perfect wisdom. We are merely the conduits. We are along for the ride.

- Is it surprising to concentrate on God's intelligence when this quality is so obvious?
- In what specific way has he shown you his intelligence? Or is there anything blocking your understanding?

Amazing God, I praise you who knows everything and created truth and knowledge from your intelligence. Thank you for teaching me to see how you want to impart your intelligence to me bringing you glory.

Why are you so afraid?

MARK 4:40

The Sea of Galilee is infamous for its sudden, violent storms. The geography of the land causes the storms. The "sea" is actually a lake and more than 600 feet below sea level, surrounded by hills. The cold winds from the mountains head toward the ocean and go across the lake. Aided by gorge-like crevices, the winds become turbulent. These storms are terrifying, and even tested fishermen keep their boats close to shore.

When I, Kathy, was a little girl in the 1950's, my family of five could only afford tent camping for our vacations. One year we found a new spot, and no one was there. We set up our equipment, enjoying the quiet.

As the sun set, a breeze began and quickly turned into a furious wind. We thought our tent would blow away along with us. Thinking the strength of the wind was an aberration, we stayed longer but the second evening the exact thing reoccurred. The next day we left.

We didn't know what we were getting into, but the disciples who climb into the boat on the Sea of Galilee do. Most of them are fishermen but even those from the "city" have heard of the infamous lake. Most likely friends had been killed on the lake. Plus, the Sea is known for being completely calm one moment and furious the next.

This story is evidence. "A great windstorm arose, and the waves were breaking into the boat, so that the boat was already filling" (Mark 4:37). There really is a reason to be terrified.

Meanwhile Jesus is "asleep on a cushion" (4:38). He is the only one not disturbed. He already told them, "Let us go across to the other side" (4:35), and he is confident his plan will be fulfilled.

The storm destroys the disciples' confidence in Jesus's care and his wisdom. Obviously, they are thinking, "How can the man who claims love as the hallmark of his kingdom *and* claim to be God be so uncaring and clueless about what is happening?" No wonder they wake him saying, "Teacher, do you not care that we are perishing?" For strong men to express such emotion and accuse Jesus of not caring reveals their distrust.

Jesus ceases the storm with "Peace! Be still!" and then asks his men, "Why are you so afraid? Have you still no faith?" (Mark 4:39-40). Maybe he also says, "Didn't I say we would cross to the other side? What I say goes."

The disciples' shock is expressed as, "Who then is this?" If only they had reminded themselves who he is—his care, love, and power—they might not have been afraid. They still should ask him to intervene but not with an accusing attitude. Jesus has taken care of them in so many different ways but to them the storm must seem beyond his care and power.

When Jesus asks us, "Why are you so afraid?" the answer often must truthfully be, "I thought you didn't care. And I forgot who you are." But we can learn to rehearse his caring and love more often as we reflect upon his care in the past.

- What other stories in the Bible remind you Jesus cares?
- Can you think of a situation, especially one God directed you to, that caused you to doubt his care?

Kathy Collard Miller and Larry Miller

Almighty God, I praise you for your caring love. Thank you for the evidence of your care in the past.

Where is your faith?

LUKE 8:25

We are back in the boat on the storm-tossed Sea of Galilee. We were there in our last devotion, but this is a different time. Again, Jesus says he and his disciples will go to the other side of the lake. Again, he falls asleep. Again, the windstorm rises, causing the boat to fill with water.

Trying to wake up Jesus out of his sleep, the disciples yell above the howling wind, "Master, Master, we are perishing!" (vs 24). They already make a conclusion all is lost but thankfully, they know who to seek as their only hope.

He rescues them and asks, "Where is your faith?" We find the word "where" fascinating. Other times, Jesus asks "what" or "why." Only a few other times does Jesus use "where" in a question. But overall, when Jesus uses "where" elsewhere, he is referring to a physical place, not the condition of the heart. This time he is addressing the condition of the disciples' hearts—where they travel away from him.

He seems to be asking,

- Where is your faith headed?
- Where are your desires leading you?
- Where will you end up?

Wonder if Jesus is contrasting the where of "we are going to the other side of the lake" to the where of "so you are already drowned and will be washed up at the shore?"

Might he be asking, "If there hadn't been a storm, were you confident we would get to the other side of the lake safely? Why does a storm make any difference if I've told you we'll arrive safely? My statement is the same. My power is the same. My confidence is the same. Where has your confidence traveled to?"

The reaction of the disciples—and us—reveals our spiritual eyes and even our physical eyes focus on our circumstances. We quickly travel in our hearts to imagine the worse.

Yes, Jesus said I'm saved, but I keep doing the wrong things. Where is your thinking heading? (Ephesians 2:8-9).

Yes, Jesus said he has a mission for me determined from the beginning of time, but no one takes me seriously. What end of the road have you bought a ticket for? (Ephesians 2:10).

Yes, Jesus said he wants to deliver me from my anger, but everything aggravates me. What disaster seems just around the corner? (Ephesians 4:26).

We all have "yes … but …" statements following where disbelief and distrust lead. Instead of clinging to the confidence Jesus demonstrates through the promises of Scripture, we follow the rabbit trail off into the forest where dangers lurk. The apparent truths of circumstances seem more accurate and real.

Unfortunately, there are times when we think God has said or promised something and we are wrong. Disappointment then nibbles at our confidence. But as we know God doesn't condemn us for our mistakes, we can grow stronger in the absolute truths of Scripture and return the ticket leading to distrust when we recognize the road is a lie.

It's not easy, but it is possible, otherwise, Jesus would not have asked, "Where is your faith?"

- Why does it seem at times Jesus is not confident? Or his promises in Scripture aren't true?
- Can you think of a time when you were confident because of Jesus's confident nature?

Gracious God, I praise you for your confidence, which assures me you never wander or sway from your plan. Thank you for building my confidence in the goodness intended for me.

What is your name?

Omnipotence. Power. No other word more accurately describes the aspect of God's nature emphasized in this story. This story must build our faith in God's immense and unlimited ability to help us.

From a human perspective, facing thousands of demons controlling one man would propel us to run the other way screaming in terror. But Jesus calmly, confidently, and accurately responds to the need of a man held in bondage and wanting to destroy himself. Whether one demon possessed him or many, Jesus is not intimidated. There is no need for "enough" power. And this work of deliverance does not deplete Jesus in any way. He regards our problems the same even if to us they feel like a "legion."

In the Roman army, a legion can have 6,000 men or more. Because we know the outcast demons inhabit over 2,000 pigs, we know there are indeed many of them.

The verb used in the story suggests Jesus "was saying" for the demon to leave, indicating ongoing instruction. We don't know why the spirits don't leave immediately, but we can surely relate. We are trying to resist but continue to be bombarded. Let us be encouraged the delay in casting out the demons doesn't mean God's power has been depleted, or he's waiting around for replenishment.

The verb indicates Jesus's command is ongoing. The spirit doesn't leave. Jesus asks for its name. Of course, Jesus knows its name, but by speaking it out loud, the demon is identified and exposed. And the realization of this lets everyone know Jesus's deliverance in a few moments is beyond comprehension.

Sometimes we need to name our problem. Worry often overwhelms us because this swirl of uncertainty and feeling of helplessness is unidentified. We need to clarify what is bothering us by asking the Holy Spirit to reveal the lies we are trusting in our mind and heart. Then we can combat the lie by identifying the characteristic of Jesus's nature or his name that will help us. We might remind ourselves he is the Alpha and the Omega, the beginning and the end, bread of life, Lamb of God, King of Kings, along with his characteristics. So many to choose from. We have explored only a limited number of his qualities in this book.

Back to the story, as the air is filled with tension and people's doubt. Then the impossible occurs. Even though the townspeople have tried to contain this dangerous man with chains and shackles, his deliverance does not bring good news. The pig farmers have lost their livelihood. They can't rejoice with the freed man nor acknowledge Jesus has made their town safer. With such a powerful action, they should have confident faith to know Jesus could reestablish their income in another occupation, even give them cash in hand. Their problem is bigger to them than Jesus's omnipotence.

Throughout all of this, Jesus doesn't have a single moment of confusion, doubt, or troubling thoughts, even when the demons resist him. Our faith doesn't have to be tossed and torn. Jesus is powerful and there is power in his name, unlimited and unending.

- Is there a different biblical story you believe more powerfully points to God's omnipotence? Why?

- What name of God gives you confidence right now for whatever you are facing?

Almighty God of the universe, I praise you for the power of your name. Thank you that you want to be glorified as you use your power to help me.

Who touched my garments?

MARK 5:30

In this story, we most often focus on the woman with the issue of blood, but Jesus's question is also used by God in the hearts of others at the scene.

The bystanders. I, Kathy, am a person who easily feels guilty and takes on responsibilities not mine. If I'd heard Jesus's question, I would raise my hand and say, "Jesus, don't look at me. It's not my fault. I'll help you find the guilty party." My response indicates I think of God as someone who is always looking for someone to blame. He's a punitive God, and I believed that lie early in life.

Jairus. This is the father who has asked Jesus to heal his dying daughter, and they are headed to his home. The father is most likely impatient and tense, thinking, *Who cares who touched your clothes? Let's hurry. My daughter might be dead soon. And I hope whoever touched you hasn't taken all your power.* Jesus halted the parade to reveal the father's belief of a weak and limited God. Jesus's purpose is not to create fear but to increase the tense man's faith by seeing the woman healed.

When the messenger arrives announcing the little girl's death, does hopelessness or faith engulf the worried father? Is he angry toward the unclean woman? After all, if Jesus is now unclean from being touched by an unclean woman, he can't use God's healing power. Yet Jesus is glorified even more by raising the daughter from the dead, not just healing her.

No longer does this grateful daddy think God is weak. He is convinced Jesus is both powerful and loving.

The disciples. The disciples hear Jesus's question and respond with fear. Like me, they are afraid of being blamed. They respond, "You see the crowd pressing around you, and yet you say, 'Who touched me?'" (5:31). They are Jesus's bodyguards. Jesus's question draws out their belief the very Son of God can't protect himself.

The woman with the issue of blood. She takes right responsibility for her action. She responds to Jesus's inquiry, which is all Jesus wants. If she had slunk away, guilty but healed, he couldn't be glorified. She rightly speaks truth, and Jesus's glorious power and love are again revealed.

Like Jairus, so often we are aware of something God is doing in someone else and make it all about ourselves. Our own insecurities, self-condemnation, or pattern of rescuing intercept God's work. As a result, we might not believe the truth about God's intentions and nature.

At the same time, God is powerful as he "multi-tasks." Jesus's simple question is used by the Holy Spirit to reveal the hearts of many. Let us pay attention to the questions he asks of those around us, but wisely only take on the ones God intends for us.

- When does God most often seem weak and not powerful at all?
- Do you identify with any of the people in this story? And what would be your response to Jesus's question?

Mighty God, I praise you because your power is limitless. Thank you for working in many lives at once. I don't have to wait in line.

Do you take offense at this?

JOHN 6:61

We are sad when we hear of someone who stopped attending church because of the sin of Christians. A pastor has an affair. A Christian businessperson swindles people. A Christian who … the examples are endless. The person leaving the church declares, "I don't want any part of a group filled with hypocrites." They are offended because their focus is on people, not Jesus.

Though Jesus is completely sinless, his words to the large group of followers has offended them, and they want to leave the "church." Jesus refers to feeding on his flesh and drinking his blood. And life coming only through him. These concepts are not only strange but seem contrary to the laws of the Torah.

Yes, they misunderstand but being offended is more than lacking mental understanding. Taking offense is a defensive protection surrounding the self and the heart—how we feel and regard ourselves and how we want others to think of us. Those in the crowd surrounding Jesus may have been thinking:

- I don't have to look to someone else for life. I'm in charge. You think I'm powerless?
- I'm keeping the Law and you're saying I need something different? You think I'm a bad person?

- You're saying I have to be a cannibal? Eating the flesh is crazy. I'm not stupid.

Of course, these are guesses, but most of the time when we're offended, we feel there's a judgment about us. We are "hurt," which is another way of saying we are insulted—put down. Someone has indicated we're less than we want to appear. For these "followers," being offended reveals they are not following Jesus out of pure motives of love and respect. They want life but on their own terms. What he can give them, not the giver.

As many in the crowd leave, they grumble all the way. Yet Jesus is immovable. We'll talk about his security in the next devotion and being secure is very similar. But Jesus's immovability about his Father's mission models strength and commitment for all followers and especially his apostles.

We believe Jesus is saying, "My followers, many will be offended and turn away. Stay immovable in the mission I've given you." Remember:

- Rejection of the message is to be expected.
- You won't be perfect, but no one is justified in being offended.
- Don't take personally the responses of others. Stay immovable in knowing I know the truth about you.
- Remember and meditate on the truths I teach you. My message is immovable.
- Spiritual growth is a process. No one will be able to change immediately. Others will struggle, and so will you.
- Growth in knowledge is also a process. Teach and rehearse the basics.

- My Spirit is the one who brings fruit within the mind and heart, not you. You are the vessel.

As the apostles will later begin their ministries, Jesus's example of not being offended will strengthen them.

- How would you describe the quality of Jesus's immovability to someone else?
- When you begin to feel drawn away from your Christian commitments, how can Jesus's immovability strengthen you?

Eternal Father, I praise you for your immovability to stay true. Thank you for the strength your Spirit gives me to be immovable in my commitment.

Do you want to go away as well?

JOHN 6:67

Without background information, we could easily think Jesus is expressing insecurity. He seems to need reassurance his disciples will remain with him and not reject him. But since he knows everything, he knows Judas will indeed betray him and Peter will deny him, so his question is not one of needing assurance. His question is intended to help his disciples examine their own hearts—as usual.

A fascinating fact is how John includes Jesus's comment identifying their small group as "the twelve" for the first time. Just envision this group on a mission like those portrayed in *The Lord of the Rings*. "The Twelve" are becoming more solidified, yet there's always the possibility of people stealing the ring for their sinful purposes. In John 6:67, in essence, Jesus is asking, "What seeds of doubt are you watering and fertilizing? Is there anything whispering in your heart why you should go away?"

Peter, brave Peter, speaks for the group (at least he thinks) and declares, "Lord, to whom shall we go? You have the words of eternal life, and we have believed, and have come to know, that you are the Holy One of God" (John 6:68-69). We would love to be a fly on the wall hearing his tone. Is his voice communicating concern for Jesus because he doesn't want Jesus to think of himself going away? Or in awe, realizing he is indeed speaking the truth and no one else has ever given him what Jesus has? Or is he trying to be convincing to the others in case a man is doubting? We can't know his tone or motive, but we know intense Peter always speaks with great passion and bravado.

Peter calls Jesus the "Holy One," and one commentator points out how the identity refers to God's transcendence. Transcendence is the idea of beyond the normal or physical. Synonyms are superiority, supremacy, predominance, and preeminence. Peter is declaring and testifying Jesus is above and beyond, transcending everything. And in this specific situation, Jesus's transcendence anchors his security. Human rejection doesn't diminish his union with his transcendent Father and his place in the Trinity. He is God and nothing will change that, especially the beliefs of those he has created.

Of course, the word "holy" is used a lot in the Bible, but the title, "Holy One" is used far less than we might expect. The title refers to transcendence because holiness, the absence of sin, applies to God alone. Curiously, the title is used by a demon (Mark 1:24 and Luke 4:34) who verbally accuses Jesus, yet Jesus confidently rebukes him and casts him out. No lack of security there.

We can grow in Christian strength because Jesus is secure. His security is "above" and "beyond" with an eternal perspective and in total control. We don't need to feel insecure if we are committed to our "above and beyond" God, who knows what is going on, controls what is going on, and originally created the whole plan.

- How would you contrast the difference between Jesus's security and human insecurity?
- Right now, what situation is creating insecurity in you? How will meditating on Jesus's transcendent security help you?

Supreme Lord, I praise your transcendency, which secures your total control. Thank you for strengthening me to base my security upon your transcendent nature.

Then are you also without understanding?

MARK 7:18

I, Kathy, once thought as an early teen I would like to be a nun. I, and a few women from our church went to a convent retreat center for a weekend of silent reflection. I loved my time there and felt close to God, even holy, because I wasn't annoyed with my brother and sister. *If only I can live in a convent, I will be able to maintain my holiness.*

At one point, I walked into the beautiful gardens, anticipating a holy time with God. I climbed onto a large boulder and began praying until I felt some pricks on my legs. I looked down and saw ants crawling all over me. I crawled down the boulder quickly with a defeated feeling. My "holy" time was spoiled.

I think we can apply my experience to Mark 7:1-23. Jesus has just been questioned by the religious leaders about why his disciples don't wash their hands before eating. The religious "purists" believe washing their hands means they are holy. They are all about cleansing the outside of the body without caring about their impure hearts. Jesus explains, "There is nothing outside a person that by going into him can defile him, but the things that come out of a person are what defile him" (Mark 7:18). Then Jesus names a variety of sinful responses having nothing to do with washing hands— and which, most likely, the religious leaders could relate to.

After the encounter with the religious leaders, when alone, the disciples ask Jesus about his parable. Even they don't comprehend. Jesus replies, "Then are you also without understanding?" (7:18). He then explains purity is not based upon what a person eats or whether hands are washed. The condition of the spiritual heart determines holiness.

Where do the ants come in? No one's "boulder" is without "ants." No one's life is without temptations and battles from within. No one becomes holy by isolating herself.

While at the convent, I thought I could be holy by avoiding temptation. I didn't care about my heart—my motives. I looked for peace being locked away in a "safe" place. But on the boulder or in the convent, I would still be *me*. The *me* with sinful desires and the ants of other sinful people. Even as a Christian with a redeemed heart, I still have a sinful nature which will only be removed at my arrival in heaven.

We would all like to go through life without temptations or challenges. Don't be discouraged if Jesus has to remind you over and over again and invite you into difficulties in order to learn to trust him more. Even the disciples don't understand.

Jesus's nature of persistence is highlighted as he explains the concept again to the disciples. He doesn't write them off as unteachable, and he never will with us. If we will listen and seek to have our heart continually forgiven and cleansed from sin over and over again—each time we encounter "ants"—Jesus will continue to teach us inwardly through his Holy Spirit.

- Why does it make sense God must be persistent since he knew he was creating imperfect humans?
- Why does it sometimes seem like God shouldn't persist in teaching you?

My kind God, I praise you for your persistence, which motivates you to continue to purify me. Thank you for showing me the importance of inner growth.

How many loaves do you have?

MARK 8:5

For one of my visual aids when I, Kathy, speak on Second Corinthians 10:5 about taking every thought captive to the obedience of Christ, I provide a rubber band for each woman. At one conference I realized I didn't have enough rubber bands. I was discouraged and disappointed. As usual, I concluded there wasn't any solution.

Then I stopped and prayed, "God, I would really like for every woman to be encouraged by using a rubber band. Please provide." Although my faith was weak, I felt encouraged. I also felt prompted to search outside. I tried not to scoff as I walked out the door. But there on the ground scattered around a tree, were rubber bands—enough to fill the gap. I was shocked and thrilled. When I told the women during my presentation about God encouraging me as he provided, the look on their faces revealed they were encouraged also.

Our God is an encouraging God. Through Jesus's question he most reveals himself an encourager to the disciples. He could have instantly and without any effort put food into the hands of the thousands. Instead he encouraged the faith of his disciples by asking, "How many loaves do you have?"

Jesus involves the disciples by asking the question. Of course, he knows how much they have. Some commentators believe this stash is the food they carry along to snack on as they walk. This is not the same miracle where a little boy surrenders his "few small fish" (John 6:9). In this case, the disciples have their own five loaves and two fish.

Jesus gently and patiently encourages the disciples beyond their comfort zone. Back in Mark 6, a similar miracle occurred. Now the opportunity to use what they learned is clear. But they still don't grasp Jesus's power fully. He knows they are weak, and he isn't bothered. He again stretches them to participate in his work and increase their faith.

For any of us parents and grandparents, we wish we could be more like Jesus's patient encouraging nature. Instead, we are tempted to exclaim something like, "I already explained that. Why can't you remember?" Although sometimes Jesus's words express a reminder like, "Oh, you of little faith," overall, he encourages them without any contempt.

Let's remember Jesus is ready to encourage us with the truth when we throw contempt on ourselves by thinking, "Why can't I learn?" or "I did the wrong thing again."

By the way, do you wonder how I instruct the women to use the rubber band? I instruct them to put the rubber band on their wrist and wear it for the rest of the retreat. Whenever a thought comes into their mind that isn't God's truth in the Bible (like, "God can't forgive me since I did the same wrong thing again"), they should take it "captive" by snapping their rubber band.

- What is your usual response when you think of God's nature as encourager?
- How are you feeling discouraged right now? Is God trying to get through the haze to give you encouragement?

Gentle Master, I praise you for your gentle and patient encouraging nature. Thank you for teaching me to resist condemning myself because you never do.

Why does this generation seek a sign?

MARK 8:12

How do you feel when you sigh? I think we primarily feel sad. Maybe the situation involves explaining something, and the person hearing us isn't getting it or refuses to understand. Sometimes there is frustration, and sometimes there's a sadness knowing if a person received and believed what we said, they would be better off.

The last explanation seems to be the situation between the Pharisees and Jesus. Right before Jesus asks his question, Mark, the gospel writer, describes Jesus's body language: "And he sighed deeply in his spirit." Whether or not the Pharisees are in the crowd as Jesus fed four thousand (Mark 8:1-10), Jesus has given more than enough proof of his credentials and they reject every one. No wonder Jesus sighs "deeply" when they ask for a "sign from heaven." Why? Because Jesus knows their motive to "test him" (8:11) and how they will reject him all the way to the cross.

His deep sigh reveals Jesus's grieving nature. Indeed, there are many situations throughout the Bible pointing to God's grief as many reject him over and over again, primarily the Israelites in the Old Testament and the synagogue officials in the New Testament.

Yet God never blames himself. His grief is pure. His motive is never about defending himself. He only wants the good of another, which is the best description of love we have ever found. Jesus knew Peter would deny him in the courtyard, yet Jesus didn't bemoan, "I'm a bad teacher. I should have done a better job instructing this loud-mouthed know-it-all." No, with sadness he warns Peter but also knows how he will later strengthen Peter with forgiveness and a new mission.

Jesus's comments are always intended to instruct and encourage, not to shame. He knows shame is not a godly motivator. Jesus's sigh is the loving concern of a heavy heart wanting to set people free—even the Pharisees. Many will indeed believe and be saved, but most will not.

But in our grief, we find it more difficult to keep pure motives. Instead, we sigh because we feel like a failure. *If only I could explain better.* We feel rejected. *They refuse to acknowledge the truth because they think I'm not representing Christ well.* The underlying longings can be mixed. No human will ever have a pure heart, but Jesus shows us his pure, grieving heart.

When Jesus asks, "Why does this generation seek a sign?" he's not needing them to explain the hearts of men. He is calling out to them and revealing the wicked motives of their closed and hardened hearts.

We can remember Jesus's sigh and his "why" question when we think we must have a sign, know the why. We must have an explanation. Just as Jesus gave many examples of who he is, he continues to call out. He does the same with us—even as he grieves because we aren't comprehending. He grieves not in disgust but in sadness. Not in shame but in a desire to draw us to greater trust in him.

- Is there any reason you think God shouldn't grieve? Explain your thinking if you do.

- Do you sometimes blame yourself when you can't make a difference in someone's life? What does your self-blame indicate about God?

Grieving God, I praise you for your grieving nature, which gives us confidence you know our struggles. Thank you for your desire to free me from blaming myself incorrectly.

Why are you discussing among yourselves ... that you have no bread?

MATTHEW 16:8

When I, Kathy, was in first grade, I was challenged to memorize the Twenty-Third Psalm at Sunday school. And being the good little girl, of course I did. But the first verse perplexed me. "The Lord is my shepherd, I shall not want." I wondered, *I'm not supposed to want Jesus to be my shepherd? I thought I was supposed to. I don't understand.* I didn't ask my teacher, not wanting to be seen as ignorant.

Did the twelve disciples wonder something similar when Jesus asks his question? At this point, Jesus leaves the disciples after they feed the five thousand. The disciples cross Lake Galilee and find him on the other side. As they join him, they realize they forgot to bring any bread. Their stomachs must be rumbling with hunger.

Then Jesus says, "Watch and beware of the leaven of the Pharisees and Sadducees" (v. 6).

In response, we're told the disciples start talking amongst themselves and apply it to their immediate problem: "We brought no bread" (v. 7).

Obviously, they immediately focus on the word "leaven" because bread is on their minds—and their stomachs. They are confused. They can't "hear" Jesus's spiritual warning about the lies of the religious teachers because they fear a possible rebuke for forgetting food. They think Jesus can't hear them, but of course, he can. As soon as Jesus talks about leaven, they think their worst fear has come to pass. *He knows the truth about us—we didn't plan well. We are in big trouble.*

The beginning of verse eight says, "But Jesus, *aware of this*, said, 'O you of little faith …' " (italics added)

Jesus was aware I was confused about the Twenty-Third Psalm, and he knew he would help me understand in his timing. He is aware the disciples misunderstand. He helps them figure it out by reminding them he just provided bread miraculously for five thousand. Bread isn't the real problem. The lies of the false teachers are.

Interestingly, Jesus, who as omniscient God knows the disciples would misunderstand, could have chosen to rephrase his words from the beginning but he doesn't. Their misunderstanding must have a purpose. It holds a life lesson they will use later.

I can appreciate now God's purpose for my confusion about Jesus being my Shepherd which gave me a hunger for spiritual understanding. And when later I figured out the correct meaning, even though I didn't know God was leading me into truth, I was not only relieved but enjoyed solving the spiritual puzzle. I like a spiritual challenge even now, recognizing Jesus builds my faith as I study the truth of the Bible.

The disciples could have saved themselves a lot of anxiety if they had spoken up instead of trying to figure out on their own what Jesus meant. He wants us to come to him. After all, he is already aware and eagerly desires to build our faith and understanding.

- Is the thought of God being aware good news or bad news for you? Sometimes it's both. Explain your answer(s) giving examples.

- Can you think of a time when forgetting God's past provision caused you to misunderstand God's intentions? How did God bring understanding?

My loving God, I praise you for your perfect awareness yet not with the intention of causing me fear. Thank you for understanding me as no one else can.

Do you not remember the five loaves for the five thousand?

MATTHEW 16:9

In our previous devotion we hear Jesus ask about their faith and now in the next verse, he asks them to first *perceive*, and then *remember* how he provided bread for five thousand. "Do you not yet perceive? Do you not remember the five loaves for the five thousand, and how many baskets you gathered?" (Matthew 16:9). Perceiving correctly who Jesus is and remembering God's actions combine to build the faith of the disciples and ours.

These two questions are a part of the same story as our previous devotion. The disciples have forgotten food. Jesus makes a comment about the leaven of the Jewish leaders. The disciples think Jesus is reprimanding them for their carelessness. And then Jesus pops the question, in fact, two questions: Do you not perceive? Do you not remember?

Jesus details his miraculous provisions two different times in impossible odds. Only miracles will solve the problem and Jesus easily comes through. The word "perceiving" refers to the spiritual understanding of Jesus being God. Only God could have done those things. Then remembering correctly what Jesus did builds persevering strength. Both are involved and interconnected.

Out of the twelve disciples, we could easily wonder why at least one of them would not "perceive," thinking, "Wait!

If Jesus did all those miracles, he can't possibly be concerned about being hungry. He doesn't need to become angry at us because he can instantly create bread again just like he did before. Obviously, he's not a one miracle wonder. He's already done more than one."

Yet evidently there isn't even one disciple who is both perceiving and remembering correctly.

If we look through the wide lens of history after Jesus questions his disciples' perceptions and what they remember, we must be even more astounded and amazed at God's work through those doubting disciples. Those "oh-you-of-little-faith" men ended up writing impressive theology of the New Testament empowered by the Holy Spirit even though in the past they couldn't perceive Jesus's simplest metaphor about the Pharisees' "leaven."

At Pentecost, here's a testimony of the general population's opinion about these disciples: "And they were amazed and astonished, saying, 'Are not all these who are speaking Galileans?'" (Acts 2:7). Obviously, they aren't well regarded. And finally, in the future, after encountering trials, obstacles, and persecution, ten of those disciples will die as martyrs.

Certainly, perceiving the truth about Jesus on an ongoing basis and remembering how he lived out who he is, must have strengthened the disciples to refuse to abandon their beliefs, whether they faced ministry problems or death. They believed God had not only called them but equipped them for the work God had chosen for them.

Whenever you are afraid you can't follow God's plan, which seems beyond your capabilities or gifting, will you perceive and remember? If Jesus, through the Holy Spirit could empower those dull-witted men to write brilliance and die martyrs' deaths, can he not provide the "bread" you need?

- What does it mean to you that the empowering God you serve enabled the weak disciples to fulfill his plan?
- What God-given assignment seems overwhelming to you right now? What first step does God want you to perceive?

All powerful God, I praise you for your willingness to use your power to enable me. Thank you for having an amazing plan for me to glorify you.

Who do people say that the Son of Man is?

MATTHEW 16:13

Jesus asks his disciples, "Who do people say that the Son of Man is?" and then, "But who do you say I am?" Unnamed disciples offer answers to the first question and Peter answers the second. Jesus starts his second one with the powerful, little word *but*, meaning there is a contrast. The disciples give the false opinions of the crowd. Peter gives the correct answer.

Every person will answer, either on earth or after death, the same question, "*But* who do *you* say I am?"

Jesus is totally assured of his identity, who he is. He doesn't need his disciples to identify him correctly. But *they* need to identify him correctly. Judas will turn away, but the rest will stay faithful. We can only wonder what Judas is thinking when he hears Jesus's two questions.

Is he one of those who participates in answering the first question: "And they said, 'Some say John the Baptist, others say Elijah, and others Jeremiah or one of the prophets'" (Matthew 16:14)? Each of these opinions shows the hearts and minds of those in the crowd.

If someone thinks Jesus is John the Baptist, they believe John rose from the dead because John is now dead. But he still isn't the Messiah. If Jesus is Elijah, he is then the prophet who was predicted to prepare the way for the true Messiah, but he still isn't the Messiah. If Jesus is Jeremiah or another prophet who indeed had a specific purpose and even did miracles, he still isn't the Messiah because every prophet died and was buried. Therefore, Jesus won't amount to much either. He's just another prophet.

Every person in all of Jesus's audiences who doesn't believe in him as Messiah and King of their lives makes some conclusion or assumption about him, which misunderstands his purpose, calling, and future results. Everyone has an opinion, but not everyone is correct. And a wrong conclusion is deadly—eternally deadly.

Most are being influenced by their own preconceived ideas of what the Messiah will be like and will do. The suffering of the Jews under Roman control motivates their desire for a conquering Messiah. The need of the hour influences them to focus on who Jesus must be. When Jesus reveals himself as the serving Savior, they reject him and think they are safe in assuming he's someone else.

We must be equally careful to not form our interpretation of Jesus's identity according to our need of the hour. We can be blinded and call him Messiah, Savior, or Lord, but we actually are not fully submitting to him. We might as well call him John the Baptist, Elijah, or another prophet. It profits us nothing in eternity.

If you haven't yet become fully convinced of who Jesus is, you have already made a conclusion, a deadly one. But you can ask the Spirit to change your perception. Jesus is completely assured of who he is. He wants you to be also.

- How is it meaningful to you Jesus is fully aware and assured of his oneness with God the Father?
- What "need of the hour" might be influencing you to resist making Jesus Lord of your life fully?

Eternal Jesus, I praise you for your identity, which never waivers. You are fully convinced regardless of what people say. Thank you for revealing more of yourself to me.

But who do you say that I am?

Matthew 16:15

Every day we answer Jesus's question, "Who do you say I am?" In each situation, challenge, or interaction, we make decisions revealing who we truly believe Jesus is. Sometimes we are just like Peter. He answers Jesus's question boldly, freely, and fiercely, "You are the Christ, the Son of the living God." Yet within a short time, he will deny he even knows *that man* who is on his way to the cross.

In the Greek, the pronoun "you" is doubly emphasized, as if Jesus asks, "But *you*—Peter—who do *you* say I am?" Jesus must be looking directly at Peter even though other disciples are there. Some of them have just answered Jesus's first question about who the crowds say he is. Jesus is addressing Peter specifically because he knows Peter will soon reject knowing Jesus three times.

Of course, Jesus knows all of Peter's life in every detail, the ways he fails, the way he speaks impulsively, and the way he will successfully choose to obey in the power of the Holy Spirit. Yet he gives Peter the opportunity to declare what he really does believe, even if Peter can't act upon it rightly every single time.

After Jesus rises from the dead, and when Peter is at his lowest, returning to fishing as if Jesus never came into his life, Jesus restores him to fellowship and gives him a huge assignment: "feed my sheep." Jesus's words are meaningful for restoration. Peter rejects Jesus three times, and Jesus tells him three times "feed my sheep."

Yet before the restoration, Jesus doesn't ask, "Who do you *believe* I am?" but "Who do you *say* I am?" There's a distinction. Believing is an inward commitment, words are the commitment lived out. Peter believes, but he originally didn't live out his belief with his words. Jesus wants Peter to know Jesus offers hope even when Peter fails.

Every day we are given the same challenge. Every choice we make reveals our answer to Jesus's question, "Who do you say I am?" When we are late for an important appointment and traffic is backed up, we express our doubt in Jesus's sovereignty by shaking our fist at the driver who cuts us off. When a co-worker takes credit for something we spearheaded, we express our doubt in Jesus's goodness by gossiping about him. When a friend deletes our social media "friendship," we express our doubt in Jesus's love by rehearsing all the horrible ways she has treated us. He isn't our Lord in the moment when we don't trust he sovereignly allows each challenge for our good, our growth, and his glory as we learn to overcome.

Yet lest we become overwhelmed with guilt and regret like Peter did, let's remember how Jesus reveals his faithfulness by restoring him. Like Peter, our actions will never be perfectly faithful to reflect our belief, but Jesus forgives and doesn't give up on us. He knows how he'll restore and equip us for the future as he continues to ask, "But who do you say that I am?"

- How do you see the faithfulness of God in Jesus's interactions with Peter?
- In what specific way do you want to not only believe Jesus is Lord of your life but confess it "verbally" through your actions?

Holy God, I praise you for your faithfulness even when I am inconsistent. Thank you for using me even though I'm imperfect.

For what will it profit a man if he gains the whole world?

MATTHEW 16:26

We recently became grandparents of … two birds. Or were we godparents? We aren't sure of the correct technical term, but we kept an eye on them in the nest as if they were our own. We don't know what the two little ones thought of us as they huddled in the nest trying to appear invisible to the huge beings who stared at them through the glass door. They weren't thrilled, but we were as we patiently watched and waited as they grew.

Of course, we tried to be as inconspicuous as possible, but because the parents chose our patio heater to set up their nest while we were out of town, we had no choice but to notice them. We watched from the first time their tiny heads showed above the nest edge until the two were so big they crowded out their parents in their tiny nest. As they grew, we wondered how the parents would teach them to fly. We watched even more closely hoping to get a glimpse.

We didn't see much going on, but one day when we weren't watching—of course—we heard a smack against our patio doors and noticed one of the fledglings was gone. Flown the coop, err, the nest.

We assumed the chick had flown into the glass and then taken off the other way. We quickly realized why the bird flew into the glass first. From the view of the nest, because it was buttressed up against a wall, the chicks had never seen the real world. They had only seen the back yard and the sky reflected on the glass of the patio doors. As far as they were concerned, they should fly toward the glass to enter the big world. Thankfully after hitting the glass, the chick turned the other way and flew to freedom. Maybe momma bird said, "Fly the other way!"

As we examine our story today, Jesus is patiently teaching his disciples about the other way—contrary to earthly thinking—when he questions, "For what will it profit a man if he gains the whole world and forfeits his soul?" His question redirects the focus and direction of those listening, not toward the reflection of what seems to be life, but the real world with sky. But they are hard-of-spiritual-hearing. As a result, he must patiently instruct them,

> If anyone would come after me, let him deny himself and take up his cross and follow me. For whoever would save his life will lose it, but whoever loses his life for my sake will find it. For what will it profit a man if he gains the whole world and forfeits his soul? Or what shall a man give in return for his soul? For the Son of Man is going to come with his angels in the glory of his Father. (Matthew 16:24-27)

God says, "Dying to self is life. Fly away from selfishness toward eternal life. Real life."

- In the biblical stories of Jesus's patient instruction, which story most speaks to you of his patience?
- When is it most difficult for you to believe Jesus is instructing you with patience?

Loving God, I praise you for never tiring of interacting with me because you are patient in your very nature. Thank you for being willing to take the time to instruct me even when I'm slow in hearing and understanding.

What do you think, Simon?

MATTHEW 17:25

The situation must be feeling dangerous. Peter has just talked with the tax collector, and Peter lies. There's no other way to say it. He tells the official they paid the tax, but they didn't. Peter walks through the door of his home where Jesus is most likely living with him and his family (at least his wife and mother-in-law). He is prepared to pour out his distress. But Jesus "spoke to him first" (17:25) and asks, "What do you think, Simon?" Might Jesus have been thinking, "I know your mind is in a whirl, but I'm going to come through for you."

Jesus must think allowing Peter to rehash everything isn't the best for him. Jesus already knows his plan. Jesus sovereignly knows what was said, how Peter is feeling, and the money bag is empty. He also knows Peter and the other disciples have been talking about "who is the greatest in the kingdom," which they will ask in Matthew 18:1.

Peter has a lot on his mind and is stressed. He might want to spare his Master embarrassment. He fears they might get in trouble. Or look bad. Or he won't be qualified for reigning in the coming kingdom, because as the host he is supposed to provide for any guest in his home. The issue seems trivial to us, but the Jewish culture highly values a host's ability to provide.

Peter is taking responsibility for the well-being of the Lord God Almighty who is omniscient and knows everything.

Re-read that sentence. Peter's response is stunningly lacking trust in Jesus, the omnipotent one who can provide at the drop of a hat. Or as it turns out, at the drop of a hook. Yet from Peter's limited view, they are on the edge of disaster, or something feeling close to disaster.

In contrast to the whirling thoughts in Peter's mind is Jesus's mind. He knows everything about eternity and thereafter but is completely at peace.

Jesus demonstrates his all-knowing peace with quick and firm decisions. Jesus gives Peter the opportunity to save face by saying they will indeed pay the tax. And here's how. "Go to the sea and cast a hook and take the first fish that comes up, and when you open its mouth you will find a shekel. Take that and give it to them for me and for yourself" (v. 27).

Peter must be thrilled. *Jesus knows and is providing. I didn't have to say a thing. How did he know?* Plus, he gets to do his favorite thing, fishing. The sea is his happy place, and he feels confident and successful there (except, of course, when a storm arises or Jesus says, "walk on the water").

Peter follows Jesus's directions exactly and presto, a shekel. *Hmmm. I guess Jesus really is omniscient and omnipotent. I don't need to fear after all.*

God wants us to think through a problem, yes, but guess what? He already knows everything and will help us to think rightly. Jesus asks Peter what he's thinking. Especially because Peter has a lot to think about and so do we all. But God already knows what we're thinking, how he will provide, and why we don't need to worry.

- Can you think of any advantages and disadvantages of realizing God knows everything?
- How can knowing God is omniscient help you in a current challenge? In what way?

Incredible God, I praise you for your omniscient character, which makes it impossible for you to wonder, worry, or be bewildered. Thank you for the assurance I am safely in your hands because you know everything.

What were you discussing on the way?

MARK 9:33

At one point or another, every parent wants to scream (or actually does), "How many times do I have to tell you? Why don't you get it?"

Jesus has every human reason to respond harshly in multiple situations. Keep in mind he is the best possible teacher and preacher the world has ever known. Everything he says is understandable and clear. But the ears of the disciples are blocked by the worried rumblings within their minds and hearts. Their fear is shouting more loudly and fueling limited understanding more convincingly than God's truth.

In spite of the disciples' resistance, Jesus is patient. After the disciples discuss among themselves which one of them will be the greatest in the coming kingdom on earth, Jesus asks his question. They must feel shocked and exposed. *How does he know what we were talking about?*

In the midst of their surprise, Jesus doesn't scream, "Peter, John, and the rest of you. How many times do I have to tell you the fulfillment of the kingdom is not a physical one but a spiritual one?"

Jesus has just clearly told them he is going to die at the hands of enemies, but he will rise again. Then we're told, "But they did not understand the saying, and were afraid to ask him" (Mark 9:32).

How sad. They didn't yet have confidence in Jesus's kindness. We can only guess at the unpleasant reaction they expected from Jesus. We all have fears of asking and exposing our ignorance based on the lies we believe about who Jesus is. Additionally, we have painful experiences from an authority figure who responded to us with frustration.

Jesus kindly takes the initiative, asking them before they bring up the issue. He doesn't want them to live in uncertainty and tension—and lies.

They arrive in Capernaum and he asks, "What were you discussing on the way?" They are quiet, maybe feeling ashamed, not wanting to reveal their selfish pride. The desire to be first in the earthly kingdom has clouded their ability to hear Jesus speak truth about the eternal kingdom.

Then in verse 35, Jesus "sat down and called the twelve" (Mark 9:35). "Gather round, guys. Let's talk." No ranting and raving. No impatience. No harsh words. He deals with their misunderstanding calmly even knowing they still won't completely understand. Then he pulls out a child from the crowd as a visual object lesson to teach the principle.

Shockingly, John says, "Teacher, we saw someone casting out demons in your name, and we tried to stop him, because he was not following us." (Mark 9:38). We are surprised John is the one speaking. Notice he says "us" not "you." We would envision him as trusting his Master's crowd control abilities. Maybe John's love for Jesus makes him protective, territorial, even for the whole group.

But any of us can succumb to putting our foot in our mouth. And when we do, we can be assured Jesus is kind and will respond with patience, just like he did with John.

- What is your favorite story in the Bible about God's kindness?

- Is it easy or hard for you to "hear" God as if he is harsh and frustrated? Why do you think so?

Understanding Father, I praise you for your kind nature, which empowers you to never respond in frustration. Thank you for looking at my heart and kindly responding with help and encouragement.

Has not Moses given you the law?

JOHN 7:19

One of many possible fears some of us may have is going to court where you maintain your innocence, but the judge finds you guilty because he doesn't believe you.

Now imagine you are standing before a judge, and he is Jesus who also acts as your defense attorney. Do you feel relief? You should. Jesus is God the Son who knows everything. He is truth and knows truth. He sees into your heart and knows what happened. As his chosen and adopted child, you are already declared blameless and forgiven (even if you are guilty). He smiles as he bangs the gavel and says, "I know the truth, but he is still innocent because I died on the cross for his sins."

In today's scenario leading to Jesus's question, the Jewish rulers and religious leaders think they can convince Jesus they aren't plotting to kill him. But Jesus, as the essence of truth, knows everything—their motives and plans. He loves them and repeatedly asks them questions to pull them out of their deceived minds and hearts.

He asks, "Has not Moses given you the law? Yet none of you keeps the law. Why do you seek to kill me?"

He is saying, "Friends, you are determined to appear to keep every law. You burden yourselves and my people. Because I'm threatening your social standing and control, you are planning on killing me. The fact I know what you're doing behind closed doors shouts to you I am God and know everything and am truth. Only God knows truth and is truth. Face the facts. Nothing is hidden from my eyes. Believe I'm the Messiah. You will receive abundant life now, and later eternal life."

But the threat is too great.

This encounter is occurring at the end of the Feast of Booths (John 7:2). Commentators believe this may also be a Sabbatical year (every seventh year). Deuteronomy 31:10-11 says,

> And Moses commanded them, "At the end of every seven years, at the set time in the year of release, at the Feast of Booths, when all Israel comes to appear before the Lord your God at the place that he will choose, you shall read this law before all Israel in their hearing."

Guess what is in "this law"? The Ten Commandments which, of course, includes "You shall not murder."

Jesus is reminding them, "In the law you just heard and agreed with, murder is wrong, yet you deceive yourselves into thinking you can murder me. Wake up."

To counterattack Jesus's truthful statement, they demonize him: "You have a demon! Who is seeking to kill you?" (John 7:20). But they are the deceived ones.

We can't judge them. Every single one of us hedges our actions at some point or another. We try to convince ourselves God doesn't see. He can't know the truth. Truth be told, he sees and knows before we act and yet is eager to forgive, cleanse and empower us to live in his power for his glory. Only being willing to give up our own glory in the eyes of others will enable us to receive such fabulous, soul-freeing truth.

- How does God's attribute of truth work with every other attribute of God?
- Does God's attribute of truth scare or comfort you? Explain which or if there is a combination.

All-knowing God, I praise you for never being deceived and always knowing and being the truth. Thank you for determining a way to forgive me through Jesus even though you know I'm guilty.

Woman, where are they?

JOHN 8:10

Although almost every theologian believes this story did occur, it is not included in the earliest manuscripts available. We are choosing to include the account because Jesus's godly cleverness is revealed. "Clever" is a tricky word, coming across as deceitful. But synonyms actually include intelligent, brilliant, skillful, astute, and quick. Those words describe the way Jesus handles the challenge he faces in the story of the woman caught in adultery.

Jesus's question comes at the very end of the story yet there's so much vital background. The Jews, who are hypocritical about their own sins, drag this guilty woman, caught in the very act of adultery, to stand naked before Jesus. Leviticus 20:10 says both the sinning man and woman should be stoned. We can easily wonder if the whole incident is set up. Regardless, she has no defense. She is guilty and deserves to be stoned.

But the religious leaders don't care about her. Jesus is their target. Their motive is to trap Jesus and destroy his growing reputation. The Pharisees craft this trick believing Jesus only has two options. If he says stone her, then the main theme of his ministry of love and forgiveness is repudiated. If he says to let her go, Jesus is a lawbreaker, dismissing sin. Either way their goal is reached: The common people will be convinced Jesus can't be the Messiah. Plus, the respect the leaders are losing because of Jesus will be restored.

Even if Jesus says to stone her, the Jews are powerless to follow through. At that time, only the Romans are allowed to carry out capital punishment. This is an empty threat of a trap. But the Jews are desperately trying to influence the common people.

In the meantime, this woman, who is shamefully exposed before all, is convinced within moments, the people will start throwing stones at her.

In the midst of the shame of the woman, the gloating of the Jews, and the gawking of the onlookers, Jesus stands confidently. He is clever, brilliant, sharp, and quick. He doesn't feel trapped by those two choices. He thinks outside the limited human box of cleverness.

He writes on the ground. Oh yes, we want to know the words. Or are they scribbles? We will never know. But his action has the desired effect. The accusers slink away, most likely feeling and knowing they are as guilty as this woman.

Jesus asks the shocked adulterer, "Woman, where are they? Has no one condemned you?"

His questions are not intended to excuse her sin. But in this particular case, the time isn't right for him to act as judge. Judgment will come later when he is the judge in heaven (Matthew 7:22).

After she answers "no one," he says, "Neither do I condemn you; go, and from now on sin no more" (John 8:11).

His brilliant intellect calmly dissolves the "trap," convicts the hypocrites, and invites the sinner to repentance and godly living—without a single moment of concern or confusion. Only by writing in the dust. How many of us would have thought of that?

- What is your reaction to thinking of God as clever? Would you rather use a different word to describe God's quality?
- Can you think of a time God helped you figure out the solution to a problem with something clever, "out of the box"?

Almighty God, I praise you for your clever brilliance as you demonstrate nothing is too confusing or unknown to you. Thank you for empowering me to think clearly about my difficult problem.

Why do you not understand what I say?

JOHN 8:43

We are lay counselors and we often use a question that helps people get in touch with their motives, "If you obey God, what does it seem like you will risk?" Sounds like an unusual question, doesn't it? Because at face value, all of us would eagerly reply, "Nothing, of course. Any time I obey God I reap life." We think we believe the premise, but then why do we choose otherwise?

Jesus's question, which is almost more a statement, is in the midst of a debate with the Jewish religious rulers. They are resisting "understanding" what Jesus is saying. They hear with their ears, but their hearts reject acknowledging him as Messiah. Too risky. They have faith in a belief system of pride, arrogance, and selfishness, which lifts themselves up and makes them feel secure. To put their faith in Jesus means they will lose those earthly rewards. Jesus's offer seems uncertain and worthless.

In one or more areas, we all want to avoid risk. To help others identify how the risk is preventing trust in God, we also ask the flip side of the question: "If you do what *you* want, what do you think you will *gain*?" The answer might bring to light their demands life must work a certain way.

Jesus is calmly debating that very idea with the Jews. After he asks, "Why do you not understand what I say?" he knows they can't answer truthfully, so he tells them, "It is because you cannot bear to hear my word. You are of your father the devil, and your will is to do your father's desires" (vs. 43-44).

Why is Satan their father? Because they do what Satan does: he murders, and his character is deceit and destructive (vs. 44). Satan has convinced his followers, the Jewish religious elite, they have life through the praise of man, the self-glory of celebrating their puny good efforts, and their worship of maintaining the illusion they perfectly keep the Law. What a heavy load to carry.

The religious leaders won't surrender to the life Jesus offers. Too risky. Too dangerous. They treasure earthly rewards too much. Jesus's offer of life through humbling themselves and admitting they need Jesus as Messiah requires death to their own pride. When Jesus says they cannot "bear to hear my word" (8:43), he means the truth is intolerable to even consider.

Thankfully, we don't have to be like those leaders. We can humble ourselves to inquire into our heart's convictions by asking questions like, "What seems so risky about obeying God in this situation? Why does my own way seem better?"

Remembering God is an inviting God, we can use his questions in the Bible as a way to explore our own lives and give up the self-centered beliefs blocking obedience. Humble yourself to see the lies you believe, and then the life Jesus offers will seem not only "bearable" but inviting.

- What are some of the advantages of remembering God is an inviting God?
- When he invites you to explore your heart, what different reactions do you have? Which one is the most beneficial?

Wise God, I praise you for your kind welcoming nature that pursues me. Thank you for never giving up on me.

Which one of you convicts me of sin?

JOHN 8:46

In John 8:46, Jesus asks, "Which one of you convicts me of sin?" Most likely there is a pause before Jesus asks his second question, "If I tell the truth, why do you not believe me?"

To say the silence between the two is a "pregnant pause" is exactly right. If the leaders can give any evidence of Jesus being less than perfect then spiritual consequences will be "born:" no meaningful death on the cross, no assurance of everlasting life, and no Christianity. The small list is only a few of the devastating ripples spreading throughout history. If Jesus is sinful.

The religious leaders are racking their brains to try to remember if Jesus responded in any ungodly way or uttered any lie. For those on Jesus's side, they are most likely fidgeting with anxiety.

The Pharisees and others have their chance. Yet no one says a word.

Then Jesus continues with his second question. "If I tell the truth, why do you not believe me?" There is an unbreakable connection between Jesus being sinless and him always telling the truth. You can't have one without the other. He is urging, "There's no reason for you to reject what I'm saying. If there is, let's hear it. Speak up. I can't hear you."

The religious rulers are extremely frustrated by their inability to discredit Jesus. They revert to name calling, as they have other times. "Are we not right in saying that you are a Samaritan and have a demon?'" (vs. 48). To be thought of as a Samaritan is the greatest insult possible. Remember the Samaritan woman? And to have a demon totally destroys any belief in his godhood. Neither works. They still can't come up with evidence. Name calling is empty of power without evidence.

Jesus's two questions reveal another aspect of himself and his Father God. He is an exact representation of pure godhood in a human body. Not only does the silence of the Jews point to his perfections, their voicelessness confirms one of the very basic foundations of Christianity: Jesus is proven the pure, sinless Son of God. Therefore, his death can be effective for making forgiveness possible for the sins of the world.

Jesus must be absolutely pure in his actions to qualify. But not just his actions, also his motives. There can be no slight impurity because there isn't any impurity in God's character. None. The Father God is perfectly holy. Angels who are aware of everything God is doing and the brightness of his pure glory, shout "holy, holy, holy." Not, "Doing okay." "A little off today." "Don't worry you'll figure it out." No. Purely and completely holy.

We humans can't qualify. Not only do we reveal our sinfulness through our choices, we learn quickly to manage our sin. To cover up our motives. We spiritually grit our teeth and force ourselves to do the right thing to look good, but our motives are not pure. Of course, none of us will ever be purely motivated, but God is. Jesus is. The Holy Spirit is. Nothing the Son of God did on earth was motivated by anything other than desiring his Father's glory and love for his created beings. Nothing. Sinless motives and holy behavior qualify Jesus to die as the pure and spotless Lamb of God for our sins.

- Has the need for Jesus's sinless motives and behavior ever been explained to you before?
- In what way do you want to become purer in your motives, even if you can't be perfect?

Perfect God, I praise you for always wanting the best and for perfectly responding. Thank you for assuring me you can be trusted to want the very best for me.

Do you believe in the Son of Man?

JOHN 9:35

Are you sometimes impatient with your growth as a Christian? Does it seem like you repeat the same sins over and over again? Are you dissatisfied with the level of spiritual knowledge you have? Our growth and knowledge seem so small at times. Certainly, God can't be patient with us. Yet God includes in the Bible the story of the blind man healed by Jesus. He wants to show us his supportive and kind patience in our transformation process.

In John 9:17, the healed blind man is grilled by the Pharisees who are on the hunt to find reasons to kill Jesus. "So they said again to the blind man, 'What do you say about him, since he has opened your eyes?' He said, 'He is a prophet'" (9:17)

This nameless man is limited in his knowledge. We can't blame him. After all, Jesus put his own spittle mixed with dirt to make mud for the blind man's eyes. Then Jesus tells him to "Go, wash in the pool of Siloam" (9:7). His eyes are still unseeing as he walks away. He doesn't know what Jesus looks like, who he is, or where he is. He obeys, is healed, and now his parents have abandoned him because they fear answering the questions of the Pharisees and being put out of the synagogue. This man is caught in a bind, without help, yet courageously rises to the occasion and tells what he knows, limited as it is.

Jesus steps in to support him. He finds the man and asks, "Do you believe in the Son of Man?" (vs. 35). Jesus gently guides him into more knowledge of himself. Here's the continuing story. "Jesus said, 'For judgment I came into this world, that those who do not see may see, and those who see may become blind." Some of the Pharisees near him heard these things, and said to him, "Are we also blind?"' (vs. 39-40).

The Pharisees are threatened by the inference Jesus makes. They know Jesus speaks indirectly of them. The Spirit is convicting them, and they resist.

The former blind man can't read (they didn't have braille) and is limited in his knowledge yet Jesus tenderly takes care of him even though Jesus is now out in the open again at risk to himself. Jesus gives the man an opportunity to learn the truth, asking, "Do you believe in the Son of Man?' He answered, 'And who is he, sir, that I may believe in him?' Jesus said to him, 'You have seen him, and it is he who is speaking to you.' He said, 'Lord, I believe,' and he worshiped him" (John 9:36-38). We can't but help envision a huge joyful smile on Jesus's face as he says, "It's me." He loves revealing himself, and he loves patiently guiding us into more truth about himself.

The next time you feel discouraged by your lack of spiritual growth or knowledge, think of how Jesus has already patiently taught you and how he will continue the journey of spiritual growth within you.

- When it's hard to believe Jesus is patient as he teaches you, what lie(s) are you believing about who God is?
- When have you judged yourself too slow in your growth as a Christian, and why do you think you make that judgment?

Precious Lord God, I praise you for your patient nature. Thank you for opening my eyes to the way you gently teach me over time.

Were not ten cleansed?

Luke 17:17

Leprosy affects every part of a person: physically, emotionally, spiritually, and mentally.

Imagine:

- You are disfigured, literally losing parts of your body.
- You must warn people, shouting "Unclean!" What a horrible way to identify yourself.
- You can't touch anyone nor be touched. You can't live with your family, have a job, or socialize with anyone except lepers.
- You can't enter a place of worship because you are regarded as cursed by God.
- You feel responsible for the health of others because you could contaminate them.

No wonder the ten lepers stood at a distance desperately crying out to Jesus, begging for mercy. They use the word *mercy* hoping compassion will fill Jesus's heart to deliver them from their pitiful condition. They have absolutely nothing of value to motivate this healer to return them to normal life. All they have are their longings but with no hope of healing ever happening. We might not be able to comprehend the longings of each leper's heart about normal life unless we have been afflicted and helpless ourselves.

I, Kathy, did experience hopelessness. I initially hurt my back but managed it with exercise. Then decades later I incorrectly lifted my infant grandson and felt the wrenching of my back. For the next nine months, I was bedridden, trying to find relief through any means from the excruciating pain. *Does God want me to be in pain for the rest of my life?* I wanted to surrender to his will but continually cried out for mercy. *Have pity on me, God!* But nothing made a difference, and my abnormal life continued without hope.

For the second time in my life, I considered taking my life. But knowing my precious grandson would grow up thinking his only grandma didn't consider him valuable enough to persevere and the discredit suicide would bring to God rebuked the temptation. Like the leper, I longed to return to my fruitful life.

But Jesus. Jesus has mercy and tells the lepers to check in with the priest. No mention of healing. They know the Torah says they must be confirmed as healed by the priest. That must mean the Miracle Worker intends to heal them. They walk away and the miraculous occurs. Can you imagine their joy, excitement, patting each other on the back, and wide-eyed amazement as they touch each other? The proof is in their smooth skin and the replacement of body parts. Normal life is on the horizon.

Jesus's merciful heart healed the ten lepers, and he healed me through surgery. I returned to normal life, like the grateful leper, with deep gratitude and giving praise to this day.

Jesus asks the one healed leper who returns, "Were not ten cleansed?" Jesus may have been asking him to recount how the others responded (even though he knew). He could be saying, "Reflect on why you didn't give into the excuses motivating and preventing them from returning. Remember their response when you don't feel grateful in the future."

The possibility of Jesus's meaning seems very real to me because God seems to continue whispering those words to me: Remember what I've done for you.

- What does God's mercy mean to you? If you are a Christian, how did his mercifulness factor into your salvation?
- In what primary ways do you feel a need for mercy? If you've never asked for God's gift of salvation, do you now? (If you'd like to hear more about receiving this gift, go to the Conclusion.)

Incredible God, I praise you for demonstrating your merciful nature by seeing my need while I was in a pitiful state. Thank you for reminding me of your gift of healing of my soul through salvation because I want to continue to be grateful.

Was no one found to return and give praise to God except this foreigner?

LUKE 17:18

In our previous devotion, we saw how merciful Jesus is, and now we are going to concentrate on his impartiality. Those two characteristics actually go together. Out of God's compassionate heart flows his impartiality to anyone who is suffering. Let's draw in some missing dots into the story and become more aware of our great God's nature.

The lepers bravely turn from Jesus who doesn't specifically promise them healing. He just tells them to see the priest. They walk away by faith. Certainly, one of them must want to ask for assurance but to ask must seem fearful. *Don't make the healer angry.*

Then the miraculous occurs. They are transformed and set free. One of them stops and pauses, looking back. Maybe another man tries to pull him along because he doesn't want to be blocked from attaining normal life. But the Samaritan says, "I have to go back and thank him." Huh?

The nine most likely thought of excuses even though they are indeed grateful. *After all, there really is no obligation. He knows we are healed and grateful. We'll find him later. Well, he didn't actually say he healed me. Maybe it was just the right time, or my obedience earned healing. None of the other guys are turning back. C'mon, let's go.*

The man's overwhelming gratitude compels him, and he falls at Jesus's feet praising God even though he is a Samaritan, a race of people who have mixed religious beliefs and are hated by the Jews. Imagine. He can actually get close to someone without being yelled at to "go away."

Jesus asks, "Were there not ten cleansed?" Could Jesus be asking, "What's in your heart motivating you to come back?" Jesus is acknowledging this man had nothing to offer, not even a Jewish connection, yet he offers his gratitude which God values so much.

Bryan Chapell in his book, *Holiness by Grace*, points out two risks the leper faced. By delaying being authorized by the priest, he risked "what has changed so quickly could change back just as quickly." [1]

Secondly, the Samaritan risks "a change in Christ's demeanor."[2]. While surrounded by his nine Jewish friends, his offensive identity remains hidden. Standing alone before Jesus, his cover is blown.

But Jesus is no respecter of people. He is impartial. Needy is needy. None of the ten deserve Jesus's mercy and the "foreigner's" identity doesn't change Jesus's compassion for a hopeless man. Jesus says, "Rise and go your way; your faith has made you well." The leper is no longer a foreigner but a part of the family of God.

This redeemed leper used to cry out with a loud voice to warn others of his uncleanness. Now his gratitude compels him to cry out to point others to the Savior.

- When you think of God being impartial, do any obstacles block your thinking?
- Have you seen an example of God's impartiality in your or someone else's life?

All-knowing God, I praise you for your impartiality, which knows our sinful status and provides our need of salvation through your Son's finished work on the cross. Thank you for meeting my needs though I don't deserve being a part of your forever family.

What is written in the Law? How do you read it?

LUKE 10:26

Today, as we look at Luke 10, we are first drawn to the parable of the Samaritan. But the chapter contains much more and the overall theme is "being" not "doing." A common phrase these days, therefore the idea seems self-evident. But to actually live in the peace and contentment of *being* is very, very difficult in our stressful world of busyness, competition, and performance.

As God in human form, Jesus understands. We take for granted the peace, confidence, and wisdom of Jesus, but we shouldn't forget he could have chosen the same stressed behavior we do. To show his sympathy, the Holy Spirit leads Luke to include three stories which demonstrate Jesus's sympathy by revealing how our human heart's desires create stress in three ways.

The first is Jesus sending out seventy-two disciples, most of them freshly chosen. They return ecstatic. They can't believe the impressive results. I think they expect Jesus to jump up and down in joy like they are. Instead, he says, "Nevertheless, do not rejoice in this, that the spirits are subject to you, but rejoice that your names are written in heaven" (10:20). We think he is preemptively preventing them from experiencing the stress of believing they must always have similar results.

In the second story, we find our question for today. A lawyer, who is an expert in defending religious law, asks Jesus, "Teacher, what shall I do to inherit eternal life?" (10:25).

Jesus doesn't answer directly because the lawyer isn't sincere. The defender of the law has kept the law and not only desires "to justify himself" (10:29), he wants acknowledgment, approval, and applause for his perfectionistic behavior. But his heart sees no need for a Messiah. (Then Jesus gives the famous story about the Samaritan showing the lawyer he is focusing on the wrong thing.)

Thirdly, we have the equally famous story of Jesus at the home of Martha and Mary. Mary completes her hostess assignments and then sits peacefully at Jesus's feet being spiritually fed. Martha frantically thinks of more she could complete and becomes angry because her efforts aren't getting the results she wants—acknowledgment of her hospitality.

All three incidents feature someone "doing" and Jesus encouraging them to "be." In all three, someone has worked hard and reaped stress. Jesus longs for them to know the peace of the security of how they are accepted by the Messiah. All three are *doing it* and wondering why *it isn't doing it*.

Our sensitive Savior, Jesus, who is sympathetic and empathetic to human feelings, is using a variety of ways to basically say, "You don't need to be stressed by *doing*. I want your heart to reside in peace by knowing who you are by *being* in relationship with me as your Savior and Lord, the source of peace." As a result of his Spirit's indwelling, we are empowered for *doing* his works as he *supplies* the drive, energy, and passion for his glory, not ours.

- When knowing Jesus's sensitivity to your needs is difficult at times, what opposite quality seems to be real instead?
- Can you think of a time when Jesus's sensitivity was very apparent to you?

Caring God, I praise you for your sensitivity, which knows our pain because of Jesus living on earth. Thank you for caring about what I'm going through right now.

For who is the greater?

Luke 22:27

I, Kathy, enjoyed being in the spotlight on stage and selling my books at events. I loved sitting at the book table even when no one was around. I was surrounded by my accomplishments. Now after more than four decades of ministry, I see the subtle erosion of my heart. When another speaker was chosen for an event, I was jealous. When I listened to a speaker, I criticized her. I wanted to be a humble servant, but my heart's pride was revealed. For each of us, pride and arrogance can seep into our hearts because we really don't trust God can fulfill all he wants for us.

Jesus's question comes immediately after Jesus wraps himself in a towel and washes the disciples' feet (John 13:1-16). The disciples wrongly believe Jesus will reward them with earthly power and prestige. Therefore, Jesus's humility is striking since this task is only performed in a household by the lowliest servant. Jesus asks them, "For who is the greater, one who reclines at table or one who serves? Is it not the one who reclines at table? But I am among you as the one who serves" (verse 27).

For three years Jesus models humble servanthood, motivated by complete confidence in his Father's ability to carry out the plan of his own glorification, which he deserves. Jesus can rightly say he has only done what the Father told him to do (John 5:19). Remember, Jesus (and God) is humble because he is rightly accessing who he is as a part of the Godhead. Jesus knows who he is and is never threatened with needing to prove himself in the eyes of others.

We can live out a similar, though imperfect, humility by not being afraid to be seen as weak, inadequate, or misunderstood. Then we can serve sacrificially.

Jesus contrasts his eternal kingdom with the proud and hypocritical example of the Gentiles whose goal is to be acknowledged as great, lord, and a benefactor. Jesus may be referring to current or past kings who took on the title of "Benefactor" even though they were actually cruel dictators.

Jesus points to his accurate representation of humility. Humility is not negating our spiritual gifts. Instead it is rightly seeing ourselves in our position in Christ and giving God the glory for anything we do in his power. Those truths are our only hope for putting more trust in God and believing he promises he will provide every opportunity and open door he wants for us.

Jesus reveals another aspect of true humility when he compliments his disciples (Luke 22:28-29) for persevering alongside him in ministry. Of course, we know they don't follow him well, and they will continue to struggle. But Jesus doesn't demand his followers come through for him to feel good about himself. God defines his worth and value.

I can't claim to never be jealous, competitive, or envious. But I can see God's work in teaching me nothing will prevent his will from being done. Such confidence in him deepens my ability to serve him out of gratitude instead of impure motives.

- Do you sometimes struggle with thinking of God as humble? If so, why?
- In what areas do you most struggle with competition, pride, jealousy, or envy?

Glorious God, I praise you for your humility, which is deserved because you only ask for acknowledgment which is true about you. Thank you for teaching me nothing can stop your plan for me.

If it were not so, would I have told you that I go to prepare a place for you?

JOHN 14:2

We have been privileged to travel for ministry to many places in the world. In many foreign communities, especially the Middle East, we observed rods of steel sticking up on top of a house as if the construction job wasn't completed. Someone explained the meaning to us. What seemed incomplete was actually anticipation and preparation for the son who would someday bring home his bride. After becoming engaged, the future bridegroom completed building their living quarters, a kind of "save the date" announcement. Although, the news of the engagement most likely has already been shared.

Since this is also the culture in Israel, Jesus is referring to something familiar to the disciples to give them comfort and peace. He has told them, as he has other times, he is leaving, and they can't go with him. Their fear must be palpable. What confusion. They have depended upon him more than they realize. Maybe they think he is abandoning them, and they are helpless. We can relate as we each think of a time when someone we needed wasn't available.

The disciples must all know men who are lazy or unskilled and delay preparing the home for their bride or create something the bride wouldn't like. Knowing their fear, Jesus is assuring them by claiming he is trustworthy and prepared, unlike the lazy men they have seen. Jesus is sensitive to their fears. He comforts them by pointing to his dependable care because he is already building their home in heaven.

In effect, Jesus is saying to us today, "Trust me when I say I'm working on top of the house. Start rejoicing now because your future home in heaven is more magnificent than any you've ever seen on earth and the setting is the perfection of heaven. Since you are my bride, I'm preparing something beyond anything you can imagine in your dreams. Have faith. There's room for you."

The symbolism of the earthly house in cultures like Israel is more than just rooms or a building to live in. The symbolism also represents the father, who lives on a bottom floor, will continue to provide everything needed and is involved, seeing what is going on. He is always there and available. On earth we might not like the idea of family living close to us, but that's because our human family is imperfect. Jesus is emphasizing a perfect Heavenly Father.

We don't need to fear the intentions of our heavenly Father who only wants good for us. We are under his care. He's in the same building, the whole earth and heaven. God is always involved and prepared in everything he intends. Jesus declares himself dependable. He has promised and he will complete the project. The disciples can trust him to fulfill his promise of a heavenly home. So can we.

Yet he isn't just dependable in providing that heavenly home but everything we need. Whatever is good for us, he promises to have already planned and to provide.

- Where else in the Bible do you see an example of God's dependability?
- What assurance does God's dependability give you, and how do you want to apply it to your current circumstances?

Abba Father, I praise you for your dependability, which you reveal out of care for me. Thank you for caring about my eternal home and every area of my life.

Did you lack anything?

LUKE 22:35

After our first child was born, I, Kathy, took her with me to the grocery store and shopped while she slept. For a few weeks, she peacefully slept in her carrier. I'll never forget my absolute dismay the day in the grocery store I looked down and saw her eyes open. *Why are you awake? You're supposed to always stay sleeping.*

I really did think that.

I don't know why it didn't occur to me the day would come when she would be awake during shopping. Did I expect her to stay asleep in the carrier when she was a toddler?

When life goes along without change, we might feel like it will always stay the same. But such a belief is a dangerous perspective, especially in the Christian life.

Jesus communicates to his disciples the correct perspective in this passage.

> And he said to them, "When I sent you out with no moneybag or knapsack or sandals, did you lack anything?" They said, "Nothing." He said to them, "But now let the one who has a moneybag take it, and likewise a knapsack. And let the one who has no sword sell his cloak and buy one. For I tell you that this Scripture must be fulfilled in me: 'And he was numbered with the transgressors.' For what is written about me has its fulfillment." (Luke 22:35-37)

Jesus contrasts two different seasons. When he sent the disciples out previously to share about the kingdom, they learned God would provide for them by giving them favor with the people they met. They weren't supposed to take anything along with them.

But now Jesus is going to soon leave them, and life will be completely different. They are going to be viewed as enemies by the authorities and both Jews and Gentiles who can harm them.

Jesus's point is not about earthly provisions but the varying assignments, the changing "journeys," God will give them and each of us as his disciples. We need to be alert and ready for whatever spiritual battle we face in a particular season. Preparation begins with the foundation of knowing God may guide in different ways than he did before. Only God is omniscient—knows everything. He doesn't expect us to.

Although Jesus's message might seem obvious, we have all felt surprised when life changes. A sudden illness. An unexpected temptation. Betrayal of a faithful friend. Even a long-term physical condition. We experience spiritual whiplash. The change exposes our hidden self-confidence, which motivates us to feel at peace. Now we must seek God's different kind of empowerment. He knows this will happen and stands ready to guide.

Even if we're caught off guard, we can remember Jesus's response to the disciples who said, "Look, Lord, here are two swords" (Luke 22:38). The disciples didn't understand Jesus's symbolism. Jesus gently replies, "It is enough" (vs. 38). Or "I understand you don't fully comprehend, but your present knowledge is enough." He knows the Holy Spirit will walk with them because he will leave. Today the Spirit shares the Father's knowledge with us.

- How is God's omniscience meaningful to you as you think of an unknown future?
- Have you ever experienced a time when a life change seemed like God was taken by surprise?

Wise God, I praise you for knowing everything and nothing takes you by surprise. Thank you for assuring me you know the plan when I experience change in my limited knowledge.

Simon, are you asleep?

MARK 14:37

Do you remember your latest holiday meal where the day involved the stress of welcoming guests, fixing a meal, eating the meal—the *large* meal—and then sitting down to watch the football game or relax while chatting? What happens? You either fall asleep or at the least your eyes are drooping. You are tired and full. Sleep seems inevitable.

Similarly, Simon can't resist falling asleep after a full and stressful day. The disciples have prepared the Passover meal. They eat the meal, which is rich and is a lengthy process with many traditions. Then the disciples are shocked to hear Jesus tell them one of them will betray him. Peter is particularly devastated to hear he, himself, will deny Jesus three times. That evening, they walk to Gethsemane where Jesus tells Peter, James, and John, "Sit here while I pray. … My soul is very sorrowful, even to death. Remain here and watch" (Mark 14:32, 34).

The most common Jewish way to pray is to stand with hands raised. But Jesus has mercy on them and says to sit. He wants to help them stay awake, but their bodies rebel. We don't know at which point Peter and the others fall asleep, but we can surely understand why.

What did Peter feel like as he suddenly awakens hearing Jesus ask, "Simon, are you asleep?" He must be groggy and disoriented. He fully wants to support Jesus with prayer, so he must have felt guilty when Jesus awakens him and asks,

"Could you not watch one hour?" In verse 40, Mark writes, "and they did not know what to answer him." There is no way they could excuse their lack of support.

All of us experience initial reactions that contradict the fruit of the Spirit (Galatians 5:22-23). We worry instead of having peace. We are angry instead of having patience. We harden our heart instead of loving vulnerably. We then have a choice whether to continue or to choose God's power for a godly reaction.

When we choose to continue in the ungodly way, the natural way, we might feel hopeless to be restored to fellowship. But let's remember Jesus also said to Peter, "The spirit indeed is willing, but the flesh is weak" (v. 38). Jesus knows the human sinful bent because he experienced temptation yet resisted. He always has a plan to provide restoration and forgiveness. When Jesus wakes up Peter, Jesus uses his "natural" name Simon, reflecting back to his old life. The name Peter represents his new calling as a follower. Every Christian at times returns to their "old name," their sin nature, but God forgives and restores them to fellowship and reminds them of their "new name" in Christ as his children, his Bride.

The three disciples want to pray yet fall asleep three times. Jesus wakes them three times. Does Peter later remember this significant number? He denies Jesus three times, and later Jesus asks him three times, "Will you feed my lambs?" How did Jesus's questions speak to him? He must realize Jesus's motive is to restore, not reject.

Our world is a broken, hopeless world. But knowing God is restoration power, there is always forgiveness and hope, and a future new heaven and new earth.

- What other words would you use for describing God's quality of restorative power?
- What area of your life currently needs the hope God can restore anything he desires?

Strong Father, I praise you for your ability to restore health to any brokenness in me. Thank you for opening my eyes to the times you have brought restoration in my life.

Judas, would you betray the Son of Man with a kiss?

LUKE 22:48

Jesus doesn't say "would you betray *me*?" He says, "the Son of Man." Commentators suggest two possible reasons.

First, "Son of Man" is the primary way he referred to himself on earth. Therefore, there's a sense of familiarity. Jesus could be urging Judas to turn away from his deception by reminding him, "Judas, you know who I am. You can't deny who I am to justify this betrayal."

Secondly, the phrase could refer to his role as judge and king. In the vision Daniel sees and records in Daniel 7, he refers to the coming of "a son of man" who has "dominion and glory and a kingdom … an everlasting dominion which shall not pass away" (7:13-14). And in Daniel 7:10, this "son" sits in judgment when the "books were opened." Jesus is warning Judas there will be judgment, and he can turn from his plan.

Even in the most horrendous betrayal in all of history, Jesus reveals his goodness of wanting the best for Judas. Jesus is modeling his command, "Love your enemies, do good to those who hate you, bless those who curse you, pray for those who abuse you" (Luke 6:27-28). Jesus can only live out such a difficult response because he is assured his life is not being controlled by Judas or anyone else. He is living out his good Father's good plan.

We also can trust God enough to respond in a godly manner in the midst of evil or mistreatment by knowing nothing is out of our good Father's control. Of course, God may direct us to speak the truth in love (Ephesians 4:15) or take other action. Jesus took action to protect himself at times. But in this instance, Jesus models strength refusing to defend himself because he knows his assignment and his good Father's intentions.

Because of his complete trust, Jesus wants to draw Judas to examine his heart. Judas's affectionate kiss hides his motive, which he believes is justified. He deceives himself as he pilfers the cash box and thinks Jesus will fight against the authorities if Jesus is arrested. He doesn't anticipate Jesus will submit. Like we've mentioned so often, he, along with the other disciples, think God is about to establish his earthly kingdom. Judas believes God isn't moving fast enough or in the right way, so he will force action.

We can so easily become like Judas, maybe not to such an extreme, but our motives can become mixed as we convince ourselves our plan is God's plan. He just needs a little help.

There is no hope for Judas, but there is for each of us as God's beloved child. If you ever think you have turned against God beyond his ability to forgive and restore you, remember Jesus's kind question to Judas. God will be glorified as you repent, showing his good nature to receive you into fellowship again.

We have a good God. Let's continue to learn to trust his goodness more and more by examining our motives and focusing on God's perfect qualities.

- What is most important to you about Jesus showing his goodness in his response to Judas?

- In what way have you recently seen God's goodness revealed in your life?

Mighty God, I praise you. There is no part of your nature not good or less good. Thank you for wanting only the very best for me and never giving up on me.

Do you think that I cannot appeal to my Father?

MATTHEW 26:53

The time has come for Jesus to be seized. Jesus is not surprised or shocked. The disciples may have feared something like this would occur, but only Jesus confidently refers to how the seizure fits in with the grand plan of salvation. What a mixture of reactions among the different people.

Peter draws a sword and cuts off the ear of the high priest's servant. The poor man most likely has no power to stop anything, yet Peter's impulsivity attacks him. Peter believes, "Do something. Anything."

In the Gospel of Mark, Mark mentions one of the followers (but not an apostle) who runs away naked because someone grabs his clothing. Commentators believe it is Mark telling on himself.

All the other disciples scatter. The scene is chaotic and confusing. People yelling accusations. The flickering of torches in the dark. Mayhem.

Except for Jesus. Jesus is calm, thinking rightly, at peace, confident, and most likely the only one talking wisely and truthfully. He is also the one who has the power to bring order out of the mayhem.

How can he be so calm? The answer is revealed in Jesus's question. Specifically meant for Peter but, of course, everyone hears, Jesus asks, "Do you think that I cannot appeal to my Father, and he will at once send me more than twelve legions of angels?" (vs. 53).

Jesus specifically and significantly speaks of twelve legions of angels. As we previously mentioned, in the Roman army a legion is comprised of more than 6,000 soldiers. In this present situation, there are eleven loyal disciples (Judas has just omitted himself from that category), and Jesus. Twelve men. If Jesus were to call more than 70,000 angels to come deliver them, each man would have at least 6,000 angels to protect him. In effect, Jesus is pointing out to Peter he believes Jesus is weak and doesn't have the needed power available.

Jesus is not weak. Jesus chooses. He *won't* appeal for help. Not he *can't*. He *can*. And his Father *would* send those angels. Jesus says, "and he [God the Father] will at once send me" (vs. 53) the angels.

But Jesus *won't* utter those words because he continues, "How then should the Scriptures be fulfilled?" (vs. 54). Jesus is committed and confident. No wonder he is completely calm. This is what he came for and what he has been living out for thirty-three years. He has known he is headed for the cross, but he won't stay there. Three days later he will rise again. The cross isn't the end. His exaltation is as he reigns at the right side of the Father.

Think again about Jesus's powerful six words. "Do you think that I cannot?"

Concentrate for a moment about your current challenge. Think of Jesus saying to you, "Do you think that I cannot … guide you?" Or "do you think that I cannot … protect you?" Or "do you think that I cannot … change a person's mind?"

What challenge would you put at the end of Jesus's six words? Might your answer reveal the possibility you believe the lie Jesus is too weak? Reflect instead on the truth of Jesus's strength to suffer for your salvation all the way to the cross.

- What inspires you about the strength of Jesus in this situation?
- Share with others your challenge and whether it has created anxiety in you because you fear Jesus might not be strong enough?

My Mighty God, I praise you for your strength, which empowered Jesus to stay the course in perfect peace. Thank you for being willing to strengthen me for the course you have chosen for me.

Do you say this of your own accord?

JOHN 18:34

From John 18:29-19:13, we discover Pilate's people-pleasing dance. Pilate's job as Roman governor in Judea is keeping peace, primarily between Romans and the Jewish religious leaders. But he also must deal with the insurrections of different zealot groups. His position also qualifies him to live lavishly as an esteemed leader.

His dance is played out as he goes in and out of his headquarters four times. In the courtyard the Jews are available to talk with him because the courtyard is not roofed. Jews can't be within a roofed room when Gentiles are present because they will become defiled—unclean. This is another of their man-made religious rules.

Pilate has brought Jesus inside to be questioned privately. Pilate says to Jesus, "Are you the King of the Jews?" Jesus answers, "Do you say this of your own accord, or did others say it to you about me?" (John 18:33-34).

Jesus knows Pilate's motives are caught in a dangerous trap because the esteem of his job is his idol. Yet, his wife warns him, "Have nothing to do with that righteous man, for I have suffered much because of him today in a dream" (Matthew 27:19).

Jesus invites Pilate to be aware of his own struggle. In effect, Jesus says, "Have you seen me do anything against the government, or are you basing your opinion upon the comments of others?"

Pilate avoids admitting he is under the influence of others, so he fights back, "Am I a Jew? Your own nation and the chief priests have delivered you over to me. What have you done?" (John 18:35). In other words, they are the ones at fault—and so are you.

Jesus is hitting a nerve. Pilate's answer is a sarcastic question with contempt to ward off Jesus's penetrating question. Then begins an important dialogue in which Jesus admits he's a king but of a heavenly kingdom of truth. "For this purpose I was born and for this purpose I have come into the world—to bear witness to the truth" (John 18:37). Pilate becomes convinced of Jesus's innocence but can't risk the Jews' angry response. Some historians believe he is a man with some scruples. So now Pilate is engulfed in a deeper trap but doesn't know how to get out.

He fights back again, "What is truth?" We don't know his intentions, but the possibilities are all defensive measures to avoid responsibility and Jesus's invitation for a heart change. Pilate figures out a satisfactory answer (to the Jews) but without knowing it cooperates with God's plan of salvation. He washes his hands of responsibility, but he will still face God's judgment.

We can be like Pilate. Every time we sin, we use some diversionary tactic to do what we want and disobey God's truth. The more we are willing to be honest about the truth, the more we will be an obedient God-pleaser.

Jesus asks us two questions for our growth. "Are you wrongly influenced by others?" And "Will you live out the truth I am the way, the truth, and the life?" (John 14:6).

- Many of our devotions refer to God's attribute of truth. Is there anything new you've learned from this story?

- What diversionary tactic do you use most often when you feel threatened by obeying truth?

Incredible God, I praise you as truth because you are never influenced by anything outside of yourself. Thank you for giving me confidence to face the lies I believe and helping me to grow in the knowledge of truth.

Eloi, Eloi, lema sabachthani?

MARK 15:34

Before his death, the last sentence Jesus speaks (as recorded by Mark) is, "My God, my God, why have you forsaken me?"—the English translation of the words of Mark 15:34.

There's really no way we can fully experience the agony of these words. We can only begin to taste a small drop of the emotional and spiritual pain if we have lost our greatest friend, or been wrongly judged and rejected, or have willingly suffered for the sake of another at great cost. Jesus is experiencing deeper suffering than all those situations because he is being separated from relationship with his Father through the most horribly imaginable thing: taking on the sins of the world.

All through Jesus's earthly life, he has been fully human and yet fully God and without sin. Therefore, he retains his relationship with his holy Father. Now, the pure connection is destroyed. Disintegrated. Decimated. Jesus has never been without the holy fellowship of his pure Father. No wonder he feels forsaken and abandoned in his humanity. Yet, he is motivated to submit to God's pre-determined will, established in eternity, in order to give glory to his holy Father.

How poignant and absolutely true are the words of one of the scribes as they talk amongst themselves: "He saved others; he cannot save himself" (vs. 31). They are right in identifying the purpose of Jesus's death, salvation, but they have one thing wrong. He *could have* saved himself. He could have called upon every angel in heaven to rescue him. He could have pulled his own hands away from the beams of the cross. He could have lifted his feet from the small platform at the bottom of the cross. After all, he had healed every other physical problem, and he had provided for every need. He is not helpless nor powerless.

No, he allows himself to be held. All for the love of his Father and those he saved by his voluntary death in submission and subjection to his Father's plan. This isn't a surprise nor a last-minute Plan B. Isaiah and many other prophets predicted everything happening now. Isaiah 53:10, in particular, must stun us with the declaration, "Yet it was the will of the Lord to crush him; he has put him to grief."

He came to die. No wonder he could say, "Father, into your hands I commit my spirit!" (Luke 23:46). This part of the plan is completed, yet the best is yet to come.

Have you acknowledged your need of such a Savior who died for your sins? Do you see how you have gone astray wanting your own way? Whether your sinful choices seem big or little, each one is rejection of God's loving will for you.

If you do acknowledge your sinfulness, then ask for forgiveness from him and make him Lord of your life. You can know God's cleansing forgiveness and begin a new spiritual journey with a loving Master and Lord. We pray you make that confession and commitment. We would love to hear from you.

- Does it make sense to you that a holy God would make a plan to provide forgiveness for his wayward creation? Why or why not?
- If you have prayed to receive God's forgiveness through Jesus's death on the cross for your salvation,

let someone know to help you travel this new spiritual journey.

Eternal Father, I praise you for your holiness, which motivates you to restore fellowship with me. Thank you for answering my cry for salvation.

Woman, why are you weeping?

JOHN 20:15

Mary Magdalene loves Jesus, alive or dead. Since Jesus delivered her from demons and she sacrificed her most precious and priceless perfume to anoint him, she has followed him with committed devotion and love. Even though Jesus says she is anointing him for his death and other times, must have heard him speak of him rising from the grave, her grief blocks her understanding and supports her assumptions this is the end of everything.

On the morning of the resurrection, Mary remains after Peter and John leave, the three of them discovering Jesus's body is gone. Her deep grief is so great even her precious teacher's dead body is important. She fears Jesus's enemies have stolen his body. When she encounters the angels in the empty tomb, she can easily turn away even though they must have been the most beautiful sight she has ever seen. She is more interested and concerned about Jesus. Then she becomes aware of another person who she assumes is the gardener. Well, in a way he is. Jesus did create the Garden of Eden and the whole concept of a garden. What a fascinating touch by the Master Scripture Writer.

The gardener, Jesus, asks her, "Woman, why are you weeping? Whom are you seeking?" Up to the end, Jesus is inquiring into hearts. Like so many other inquiries into a person's heart, Jesus isn't putting her down because she is weeping or seeking. He sees her devotion and love for him.

He chooses her as the first person he addresses after his resurrection. The resurrection account must be true because a Jewish man would have never given a woman the honor.

Many reasons account for her not recognizing Jesus. Her eyes are swollen from crying. The possibility the man could be Jesus is inconceivable because Jesus is dead. She saw his body laid in the tomb. Also, it is still dark as the day dawns.

What she experiences becomes her truth but some of her beliefs are lies and others are incomplete. On the one hand faith is developed with experience and knowledge. But what we experience and learn can become assumptions, which block the identifying of lies or incomplete truth. Mary believes the truth about Jesus as her teacher, but she believes he will forever be dead.

When she asks the "gardener" about the body, she never uses Jesus's name to identify him. "Sir, if you have carried him away, tell me where you have laid him, and I will take him away" (John 20:15).

Three times she refers to Jesus as "him" and assumes everyone must know who she's talking about. He is the only person of interest to her. He is extremely and ultimately important to her, and for someone else to not be as equally enthralled is beyond comprehension. In fact, she believes she will have the power to carry his dead body to a safe place. She will do anything for her teacher. Oh, that we would seek Jesus with such passion and commitment. To think of nothing as enthralling as him.

Then he says her name and her false assumptions are corrected with truth.

- How can knowing God is full truth give assurance even when we are limited by our assumptions?

- Can you think of a time you realized your assumption was incorrect and God taught you truth more fully?

Amazing God, I praise you for your nature of truth and how everything you do is based in truth. Thank you for wanting to enlarge my understanding and knowledge with greater truth.

Was it not necessary that the Christ should suffer these things?

LUKE 24:26

Several years ago, I, Larry, first began to study and understand the importance of examining all of the Bible to recognize references to Jesus. I'd never understood how significantly Jesus is revealed both in the New and the Old Testaments. As I shared with Kathy, she also began to appreciate the joy of seeing Jesus throughout Scripture.

In this passage as Jesus encounters two of his followers on the road to Emmaus, we comprehend how important such study is to Jesus. Jesus hides his true identity from them, maybe to prevent them becoming so stunned and full of joy they won't be able to listen fully to his history lesson. Verse 27 tells us, "And beginning with Moses and all the Prophets, he interpreted to them in all the Scriptures the things concerning himself."

The three-word phrase "all the Scriptures" is absolutely and remarkably noteworthy. Jesus wants his presence to be seen all the way from the Genesis account through the end of the Old Testament ending with Malachi 3:1.

Many people believe the God of the Old Testament is different than Jesus in the New Testament. The Old Testament God is angry. Jesus is full of love and grace. But those are misconceptions. The Trinity is the same even as they have different functions. Our understanding may be skewed but their overwhelming presence as a whole throughout Scripture is not skewed. We just need to study with a lens recognizing God as a whole, even if the appearance we "see" seems different.

For Kathy and me, this awareness makes a difference in our lives. We are more convinced of the truth of who God is as the Trinity and their involvement in our lives. And as we've studied the different qualities comprising God's nature, no characteristic is more or less in who God is.

At times, God might be emphasizing a particular quality of his being. God is sensitive to the need you are facing. He knows what will encourage you and be the beacon for pointing you to the truth about himself. You will be able to share with others more about God in powerful and truthful ways.

Jesus first asks the couple, "What is this conversation that you are holding with each other as you walk?" (24:17). Jesus is teaching them to practice telling the story they will share numerous times in the future. At this point, their testimony is powerful, but it is incomplete. Jesus broadens their understanding starting at the beginning of the Scriptures and telling them everything which points to him.

Because the Holy Spirit is dwelling within a Christian, he is doing the same thing, teaching us the truth about God based on the totality of Scripture. We can't encourage you enough to study both the Old and New Testaments and look for sightings of God the Father, God the Son, and the Holy Spirit. Your spiritual life will be fuller and richer. And you will understand God's omnipresence in all of history.

- What is meaningful to you about the importance of recognizing the presence of the Trinity throughout Scripture?

- How would you like to study the whole Bible with the goal of identifying each aspect of the Trinity?

Glorious God, I praise you for your presence in all of Scripture without any discrepancies. Thank you for your desire to reveal yourself to me in truth.

Why do doubts arise in your hearts?

Luke 24:38

The sounds within the room are most likely hushed with everyone murmuring. At times a voice or laugh rises above the clamor. Some of the apostles, Mary, and Cleopas and his friend have told their stories over and over again. What should they do next? They ask each other, "What do *you* think?" Every single aspect of what they are experiencing is totally unheard of. Totally unexpected. Totally surprising. Totally confusing.

The door is locked. Of course, everyone in the room expects danger. This is not a safe place. There is no safe place. If there's a knock at the door, everyone hushes and looks around at each other with terror. Their eyes ask, "Friend or foe? What will happen? What should we do?"

Then Jesus appears out of nowhere. Suddenly. Unexplainably. He says, "Peace to you!" (24:36). Peace is the most foreign emotion for them right now. Wonderment, tension, joy, excitement, fear, confusion, expectations—a muddle of feelings swirling through them all.

Jesus knows and is sensitive to their state of mind and heart. He has told them to be at peace other times, but this must be the most distressed they have ever felt over the three years of following him. Peace? When a ghost is suddenly among you? No way. Luke writes, "But they were startled and frightened and thought they saw a spirit" (vs. 37).

Jesus assures them they can be at peace, and he is not a spirit. He encourages them to not be troubled or doubt. He extends his pierced hands. He points to his pierced feet. He invites them to touch him, explaining he has flesh and bones. They can't comprehend what they are seeing. In the midst of their joy and marveling, he asks for food to eat. He wants them to know he is real, and they don't need to fear.

And then just like he did on the walk on the road to Emmaus, he instructs the whole group about himself from "the Law of Moses and the Prophets" and how "the Psalms must be fulfilled." And because he is sensitive to their human confusion, "he opened their minds to understand the Scriptures" (vs. 45). Can't you just see Cleopas and his companion nodding and whispering, "Yes, he told us also. Remember? Do you understand now? See? We aren't crazy."

And in a further sensitive response, he assures them they will not be alone. His Spirit will come and clothe them with power from on high.

Even though it is impossible for us to fully feel these followers' emotions, we can recognize Jesus's sensitivity. His caring. His concern.

God, your loving Heavenly Father, and Jesus who intercedes for you before the throne, is as sensitive, caring, and concerned about every aspect of your life. He assures, confirms, gives evidence, reminds, encourages, and provides support. Because Jesus experienced the challenges of daily life as a human, he sensitively knows how to provide everything you need.

- What part of this story of Jesus showing his sensitive nature is most meaningful to you?
- Can you think of a time you concluded God wasn't sensitive to you? What do you believe now?

Almighty God, I praise you for your sensitive nature, which cares about every aspect of my life. Thank you for working on my behalf because you care for me.

Have you believed because you have seen me?

JOHN 20:29

Wouldn't you like to know what the disciples and followers, who had seen Jesus, were thinking when doubting Thomas said, "Unless I see in his hands the mark of the nails, and place my finger into the mark of the nails, and place my hand into his side, I will never believe" (20:25).

Did they laugh? Did they scowl? Did they tease him? Did someone say, "You think we're lying about seeing Jesus? You don't believe *any* of us?"

The level of his doubt is very serious considering reliable disciples are urging him to believe them. It might not be an appreciated characteristic, but Thomas is not easily swayed. Yet we wonder with such remarkable testimonies, what kind of a man has such depth of doubt?

In contrast, John also includes Thomas's comment when Jesus says he will go to Bethany because Lazarus is sick. Thomas urges the other disciples, "Let us also go, that we may die with him" (John 11:16). That took courage and commitment. No doubt there.

The only other reference to Thomas (other than his name included in groupings of disciples) is John 14:5, when Thomas asks Jesus, "Lord, we do not know where you are going. How can we know the way?" Thomas wants details and assurance.

Thankfully, Jesus appears again, shows him the marks, and challenges him, "Do not disbelieve, but believe." Thomas replies, "My Lord and my God!" (John 20:28). Thomas is either all in or all out.

Jesus graciously accommodates Thomas's need for proof. We don't know where Jesus has been for the eight days since he last appeared. But he isn't obligated to appear again. Everything Jesus does always has a purpose and obviously Thomas has not been rejected because of his reticence.

As Christians, we can be grateful for Jesus's accommodation of Thomas. So often in the Christian community, anyone who doubts is told to "just believe" or "take it on faith." Some even think no one should doubt at all. Sadly, a "doubting Thomas" might be criticized and become discouraged, even doubting he is a Christian. Often, we respond in unloving or impatient ways to someone's doubts because we feel inadequate to help them and to convince them of truth.

But Jesus's gentleness can guide us to realize some people are just more thoughtful and want to be sure of what they believe. They might be very passionate in their belief and in their doubt, creating a pendulum response.

Thomas is one of those. He has honest intensity. When he urges the disciples to go with Jesus to possibly die with Jesus in Bethany, he is revealing his faith and commitment. Any one of us can swing from faith to doubt. Jesus can show us how we can moderate those swings and become more consistent. Involvement in the Body of Christ is essential. Let's make the Christian community a safe and welcome place for any, especially doubters, like Jesus did.

- Does thinking of God as accommodating speak to you in a positive way or seem inaccurate?
- To what degree are you like a "doubting Thomas"? What response have you received from others, especially Christians, when you express doubt?

Gentle God, I praise you for your accommodating nature, which responds to my needs in a gracious way. Thank you for your tenderness toward me when my faith is small or weak.

Do you love me more than these?

JOHN 21:18

No one wants to be reminded of their sinful choices. Satan, our accuser (Revelation 12:10) loves to use guilt and shame to fuel our self-hate and distrust of God. His motive is to convince us God can't possibly still love us.

At the point of this encounter between Jesus, Peter and other disciples, Jesus will pursue Peter with steadfast and laser-focused inquiries into Peter's still-hurting heart. Jesus continues Peter's healing process by setting up circumstances and choosing words reminding Peter about various aspects of the past:

- Peter denies Jesus three times. Now, Jesus asks Peter the same question three times and assures him with the same statement three times.
- Peter is called as a follower by Christ after Jesus's miracle of providing fish. Now, Jesus provides a boatload of fish.
- Peter denies knowing Jesus in the setting of a blazing fire. Now, Jesus welcomes the group to the campfire as fish are browning on a blazing fire.

Jesus asks Peter, "Do you love me more than these?" giving him an opportunity to reflect on his boastful claim, "Though they [other disciples] all fall away because of you, I will never fall away" (Matthew 26:33).

These important interactions continue the work of healing in Peter's soul. If we were Peter, we most likely would think, "Does it really take all this to heal? I don't want to review my sin. I think I'm over feeling bad." But Jesus knows he is not, and sometimes we aren't either.

Jesus's persistence reaps the reward—a change in Peter's heart. Peter's interaction after Jesus's third inquiry is different than ever before.

Peter is grieved because he [Jesus] said to him [Peter] the third time, "Do you love me?" and he said to him, "Lord, you know everything; you know that I love you." Jesus said to him, "Feed my sheep" (John 21:16).

A blustery Peter from the past would have passionately defended himself and taken impulsive action demonstrating his love. But this time, Peter acknowledges Jesus knows everything, trusting his Master knows his heart's devotion for Jesus. Peter no longer has to prove his love.

Can we receive the Holy Spirit's work of healing even as he reminds us of past sin? We might not be as spiritually healthy and healed as we think. Satan calls attention to the needed places of healing, accusing us and wanting to defeat us. His motive is to destroy our confidence in God's forgiving and healing power.

God's motive is the opposite. God does not intend to shame us but to steadfastly pursue our heart's need of greater healing. As we face our sin and receive forgiveness and cleansing, our pride is shattered. Our ability to tell others of our Master's loving acceptance increases. Our compassion for others empowers us. Our gratitude for salvation blossoms. Our praise for God's perfect attributes deepens our relationship.

In the case of Peter, he is no longer convinced he is better than others, and he becomes a powerful leader in the church, giving the first sermon ever about Jesus on the Day of Pentecost.

When you remember your ungodly past, don't let Satan use it for harm. Trust God to bring deeper healing.

- Why do you think followers of Jesus sometimes resist God's steadfast inquiries into their hearts?
- How do you first respond when the Holy Spirit brings up a past sinful choice? How do you want to respond, believing and trusting God will heal you more?

My Lord God Almighty, I praise you for your steadfast nature, which never gives up inquiring into my heart for my good. Thank you for helping me see the difference between Satan's evil motives and your loving motives.

What is that to you?

JOHN 21:22

Jesus has just communicated to Peter his forgiveness and the restoration of their relationship, along with guidance about Peter's future ministry. Here's the next scene:

> Peter turned and saw the disciple [John] whom Jesus loved following them, … When Peter saw him, he said to Jesus, "Lord, what about this man?" Jesus said to him, "If it is my will that he remain until I come, what is that to you? You follow me!" (John 21:20-22)

Peter can't resist being competitive and comparing himself to John. We know Peter is impulsive and self-confident. And now he isn't satisfied with his own assignment. He also wants to know about the Master's plan for John.

In that question Jesus points to his own discerning nature. He never second guesses himself. He knows the end from the beginning. He can discriminate between a good plan and a bad one. And he judges correctly what is best for every person.

I, Larry, am known as a person who rarely second-guesses himself. Just ask Kathy. Kathy, on the other hand, tends to second-guess herself. She will admit to that. No wonder God put us together. I've realized I should be willing to question my motives, and Kathy has become more decisive. Unfortunately, my confidence in my decisions was required and honed as a cop. If I hesitated or lacked confidence to respond quickly, lives could be at danger.

One night I chased a man who was thought to be breaking into houses through a backyard. As he tried to climb over a fence, he reached back. In the dark I couldn't see what was in his hand, yet I hesitated to pull the trigger even though I had every reason to assume he was pointing a gun at me. It turns out he was reaching for his glasses, which had fallen off his face. Even though God graciously prompted me to spare his life, I berated myself for my hesitation. I could have put myself and my fellow officers in danger.

I became more determined to never hesitate or question myself—at the harm of our marriage. If Kathy questioned me, even with good intentions, I defended myself. My God-given confident temperament had become a control strategy. Thankfully, God discerns my sin and is teaching me to be willing to evaluate my thinking and be more humble.

Peter is questioning his Master's discernment. "What about John, Lord? What's going to happen to him?" Although his question might not seem ungodly, maybe just curious, Jesus sees Peter's motive to know about other people, possibly with the desire to control another person or protect himself.

The Master says to Peter, "What is that to you?" He says the same thing to us. "I know the best plan for that person, look to yourself to follow me. Trust my discernment and keep your eyes on me. You'll have enough to work on in yourself without wondering about someone else."

As we each surrender to God's wise plan, the Body of Christ will be more harmonious, effective, and bring more glory to God.

- What does it mean to you God never second-guesses and is always wisely discerning?

- To what degree do you second-guess yourself (or someone else) and how would you like to take one step to trust God's discernment?

Amazing God, I praise you for your discerning nature which knows the intentions and motives of my heart and everyone else. Thank you for giving me permission to release control over others and just focus on allowing you to change me.

Saul, Saul, why are you persecuting me?

ACTS 26:14

The only direct communication we have from Jesus after his ascension is on the Damascus road as Jesus's voice calls out to Paul, then known as Saul, a persecutor of the early church. Jesus appears to him, asking, "Saul, Saul, why are you persecuting Me? It is hard for you to kick against the goads" (Acts 26:14).

The first sentence indicates Jesus identifies with his church, the Body of Christ. Technically, Saul hasn't been persecuting Jesus at all. He has been persecuting Christians. But Jesus basically says, "If you are persecuting my beloved church, then you are persecuting me."

We can be comforted as we know Jesus identifies with our pain when we are misunderstood and given any negative feedback about our faith. Jesus is in our shoes. Even though persecution and his sacrificial death doesn't make him take it personally, he, in a sense, takes it personally when his people, his followers, are hurt or harmed. He stood up against Paul and he stands up for us. Jesus is protective.

How amazingly strengthening. We all are not alone when we feel slighted, ignored, or considered ignorant if someone rejects Jesus when we share about him. Their reaction isn't about us. They are resisting Jesus. He's by our side and we can be strengthened to continue sharing as he leads.

The second sentence by Jesus, "It is hard for you to kick against the goads," is like asking, "Why are you persecuting me when you are the only one being hurt? Not smart."

The phrase about the goads is not included in most original copies of Luke's account in Acts 9. (Luke wrote Acts). Paul adds the phrase when he gives his testimony of salvation to King Agrippa in Acts 26. Evidently, Luke doesn't think the phrase is important or else Paul is trying to make a particular point to King Agrippa. Maybe Paul is saying to the King, "What are you? Stupid? Believe in Jesus and be smart. Believing is in your best interests."

"Kicking against the goads" is based on a proverb used by Latin and Greek writers. It refers to sticks with pointed pieces of iron fastened to them and are used to prod the cattle as they plow a field. If an ox rebels and kicks against the prod, it will give itself pain. Not smart.

Jesus is seemingly encouraging Paul to look out for himself and stop hurting himself. We could each ask ourselves the same thing. Maybe we'll be more obedient if we ask ourselves, "What? Are you stupid? Why do you keep choosing the same disobedient things when resisting the Holy Spirit's empowering is not in your best interests?"

We often disobey because we think we have to protect ourselves. Our protection isn't even effective. But Jesus is who can and wants to protect us. He wants the best for us. When we disobey like Paul was, he says, "I know what's best and this isn't it." He says the same thing to us and assures us he will protect us as needed.

- What do you think causes someone, even yourself, to not believe God's protective nature?
- How can you trust in God's protection more in your current struggle?

Amazing God, I praise you for your protective nature. Thank you there is no one more capable than you who can protect me and judge what is for my best.

CONCLUSION

Congratulations. You've completed your one-hundred-day journey of becoming even more aware of God's qualities and your own motives. We pray and hope you sense a greater knowledge of who God is in truth and how he wants to reveal himself to you. We also pray you are more aware of your own desires which may or may not direct you to trusting God. May you be assured your loving heavenly Father wants to purify your motives more and more for your good and his glory.

Here are some practical ideas for continuing your spiritual journey in exploring God's qualities.

Begin and continue adding to a list of God's qualities as you become aware of them. Keep the list in a prominent place where you will see it frequently.

Categorize your list, either on the same sheet, or on another list. Write the alphabet down the left side. Alphabetize God's qualities by each appropriate letter.

Use the alphabetized list as a means of praising God. For instance, on Monday, meditate on the "A" words describing God. On Tuesday, the "B" words. And continue on for a total of twenty-six days.

Find Scripture verses describing God's qualities and write them on file cards. Distribute and tape those cards to various surfaces within your home or workplace.

Whenever you are feeling tense, angry, withdrawn, or any other response, which is not the fruit of the Spirit (Galatians

5:23-24), ask yourself, "What am I thinking or believing about who God is right now? Is this quality true about God or is my thinking based on a lie about him?"

Remember and rehearse the times God has shown you his true qualities. Praise and thank him for those times.

In our book we talk about being reconciled to God through Jesus Christ who died on the cross for your sin. If you now know you are not reconciled with your Creator and want to change that, recognize your sin and place your faith in Christ's work on your behalf on the cross. There is nothing you can do to earn God's gift of eternal life. Surrender, pray and ask God to forgive you and thank him for saving you. We would love to hear of your decision to do this.

Thank you for reading our book. We have gained much from sharing with you. Ask our wonderful Lord to open the eyes of your heart to recognize the perfections of his nature and how he wants to strengthen your ability to desire his glory.

We would love to hear from you. Please connect with us at www.KathyCollardMiller.com.

ENDNOTES

1. Bryan Chapell, *Holiness by Grace: Delighting in the Joy That is Our Strength,* (Wheaton, Il.: Crossway Books, 2001), 29.

2. Chapell, *Holiness by Grace*, 30.

BIBLIOGRAPHY

Believer's Bible Commentary, William MacDonald, Thomas Nelson Publishers, Nashville, 1995.

The Bible Knowledge Commentary, New Testament, John F. Walvoord, Roy B. Zuck, Victor Books, Scripture Press Publications, Inc., USA, 1987.

The Compete Word Study Dictionary New Testament, Edited by Spiros Zodhiates Th.D. AMG Publishers, Chattanooga, TN,1992.

The Greco-Roman World of the New Testament Era, James S. Jeffers, Intervarsity Press, Downers Grove, IL, 1995.

Holiness by Grace, Bryan Chapell, Crossway Books, Wheaton, IL, 2001.

Life Application Bible, Tyndale House Publishers, Inc. Wheaton, IL. And Zondervan Publishing House, Grand Rapids, MI, 1991.

The Narrated Bible, Narration by F. LaGard Smith, Harvest House Publishers, Eugene, Oregon 97402, 1984.

Parallel Bible Commentaries, The Bible Hub, Online Parallel Bible Project, www.biblehub.com, P.O. Box 50, Glassport, PA, 2020.

Vine's Expository Dictionary of Old and New Testament Words, W.E. Vine, Fleming H. Revell Company, Old Tappan, NJ, 1981.

ABOUT THE AUTHORS

Larry and Kathy Miller married in 1970 and anticipated a "marriage made in heaven" kind of relationship, especially since Larry had brought Kathy to his church where she became a Christian. But their marriage disintegrated within seven years. Kathy took her anger out on their two children, and Larry worked more. But God healed and restored their relationship and family. They didn't realize God intended to use their pain by birthing a ministry for each of them and for them as a couple.

Larry is a retired police lieutenant from Huntington Beach, California, and frequently speaks for men's groups, preaches at church services, leads Bible studies, and is an elder at their church, Redeeming Grace Church, Palm Desert, California. He has written several books including *Men of the Bible*, and with Kathy has written numerous books including *Never Ever Be the Same: A New You Starts Today*.

Kathy is best known for her practical biblical teaching with vulnerable sharing, humor, and motivation woven throughout her speaking and writing. Kathy's articles have appeared in hundreds of magazines and online sources. She has appeared on many radio and television programs including The 700 Club, often with Larry.

Her first book telling her story of God's work to deliver her from being a child abuser was published in 1984 and now has been revised and expanded as *No More Anger: Hope for an Out-of-Control Mom*. She is the best-selling and award-winning author of over fifty-five books, which feature a full array of nonfiction genres including Bible studies, Bible commentaries, and Christian living topics, and has also been an editor of compilation books. Some of her other books are *Pure-Hearted: The Blessings of Living Out God's Glory* and the multiple books in her women's Daughters of the King Bible study series.

Since their ministry began in 1978, Larry and Kathy have been in awe of God's plan to develop their ministry with a world-wide impact speaking both in the United States and around the world in Indonesia, China, Poland, Greece, and other countries. Kathy and Larry often write and speak together, especially at marriage events. They are also lay counselors.

The Millers live in Southern California and are the parents of two and grandparents of two. Connect with them at:
www.KathyCollardMiller.com
www.facebook.com/KathyCollardMillerAuthor
www.twitter.com/KathyCMiller

BOOKS BY KATHY COLLARD MILLER
with Elk Lake Publishing, Inc.

Pure-Hearted: The Blessings of Living Out God's Glory

No More Anger: Hope for an Out-of-Control Mom

Daughters of the King Bible study series:

Choices of the Heart: ten lessons about the women of the Bible, contrasting two different women of the Bible about different topics.

Whispers of My Heart: ten lessons about prayer.

At the Heart of Friendship: ten lessons about different aspects of relationships.

Heart Wisdom: ten lessons about different topics covered in the biblical book of Proverbs.

Made in the USA
Columbia, SC
12 June 2020